FROM
GLASGOW
TO THE
WORLD

The Institute buildings

FROM

GLASGOW

TO THE

WORLD

The story of the
Bible Training Institute
and its successors

Rose Dowsett

LOXWOOD PRESS

ISBN 978-1-908113-66-5

Published 2023 by Loxwood Press.
50 Loxwood Avenue, Worthing, West Sussex BN14 7RA
Tel: 01903 232208

Printed & designed by Kenads Printers, Worthing

CONTENTS

Preface

George Verwer writes:

The global Bible College Movement has been and still is one of the strongest forces for holding to God's Word and reaching the world with the gospel. This was true of BTI. My mind jumps back to them letting me speak there even when I first came many at that time were sceptical about me and OM. It became one of our best recruiting grounds, and only eternity will tell the story of many dozens who went on OM, many of whom became long-term workers.

We need today men and women who know the Bible, who are grounded in the Word of God. Just the opportunity to get to know the Bible to me is so important and shouts out so loudly the importance of a Bible College education. Whether you go into a marketplace ministry with a bank or a company, or whether you go out into ministry of a mission in some distant country, to have a knowledge of the Word of God is extremely important whatever your future may be.

As a graduate of Moody Bible Institute, I know how rich and important a Bible college experience is. In our day, many churches and denominations have their own Bible Colleges, but the roots go back to places like BTI.

George Verwer, founder of Operation Mobilisation (OM) and Send the Light

Peter Rowan writes:

It would be difficult to over-estimate the pivotal role played by the Bible College movement in training workers for global mission. The legacy of that movement continues – not only the men and women who trained at such colleges and are now leading ministries, organisations and mission agencies, but also in the colleges and institutes scattered across the globe that were modelled on colleges such as the Bible Training Institute.

The BTI/Glasgow Bible College had close connections with missions in China and Asia. It was no surprise therefore that the China Inland Mission/OMF received great numbers of graduates from the college – graduates who emerged with a passion for the Bible, for evangelism, for missionary service in East Asia, and, also a strong factor in the Bible College model, prepared for service in an inter-denominational and international mission.

The typical Bible College training package was delivered by a faculty of reflective practitioners, men and women who may not have had academic qualifications (though many had, even to the highest level), but had credibility because of their years of varied ministry experience and proven gifts in teaching and training. Studies and academic work were important, but spiritual formation in the context of community was often at the heart of the Bible College experience, as was practical, hands-on, church-based ministry.

As one of the very first Bible Colleges in Britain, the BTI model would have been influential, not least in the emphasis given to missionary training. Cross-cultural training became a strong feature in most colleges throughout the twentieth century. My own journey in mission has an indirect link to the Bible Training Institute/Glasgow Bible College. I may be biased, but one of the strongest mission studies programmes offered in the 1980s was to be found at Moorlands Bible College. The programme director was Dr John Davis, a graduate of BTI, and, as it happened, a former OMF missionary!

Peter Rowan, National Director UK Overseas Missionary Fellowship (OMF)

Introduction

AN AFRICAN pastor came bounding up to me at an international conference. "Have you heard of the Bible Training Institute in Glasgow?" he asked. "Yes, indeed," I replied. "In fact, I taught there for about 18 years. Why do you ask?" "Well," he said, "my grandmother came to faith in Jesus Christ as a result of friendship with a graduate from there, many years ago now, and she passed down her faith to my father and then to me. In fact, she became a catalyst for her whole village turning to Christ."

The following day, both an Indian and a Brazilian came to me with the same question and very similar stories. Later, in Australia, several people approached me with the same account of how they or their forbears had come to faith. I already knew, through my own mission, OMF International, that many former BTI students had gone to China until that was no longer possible from 1951, and then to numerous other Asian countries.

Clearly here was a story that needed to be told! As I dug into records and chatted with many individuals, I found so much that made me want to sing "Thank you, Lord!"

This account is of necessity only part of the story. I could only select a few of the many stories that could have been told – and there are hundreds more that I don't know anyway. I have also chosen to focus largely on the impact of BTI graduates, and those of its successors, Glasgow Bible College and finally International Christian College, on the spread of the Christian gospel around the world, from BTI's inception in 1892 till the closure of ICC in 2014. Many, many graduates also made an enormous contribution to churches and Christian agencies here in the UK. Many also made their mark for God in secular employment, or as home makers, or as members of their local churches. There is no ranking of importance in the heart of God in these different occupations – they are all precious arenas for living out a vibrant faith – even though my own calling as a cross-cultural missionary and as a student of the world church has made the global story the main focus of what I have written.

I could have used only stories from CIM and OMF history, there are so very many, but I have tried to draw on others, too, in the interests of integrity. It has sometimes been harder for me to track those down, so I ask your forgiveness if some ministry dear to your heart does not appear.

BTI/GBC was part of a wider Bible college movement, which has been used by God in remarkable ways. I am grateful to two friends, George Verwer, founder and lifetime leader of Operation Mobilisation, and Peter Rowan, National Director of OMF International, UK, for setting that scene, against which this story of BTI/GBC stands.

Rose Dowsett

1
How it began

A SMALL, rather tubby man was standing balanced on a carriage drawn up outside the recently opened Kibble Palace, an impressive vast circular greenhouse for tropical plants, at one edge of the Glasgow Botanic Gardens. Before him was a huge throng, several thousand strong, of men and women, listening intently as he spoke.

It was a chilly spring evening at the end of May 1874, but nothing would have kept them away. For the man speaking was the American evangelist, Dwight L Moody, and this was to be his final night in Glasgow. It had been planned that this last meeting should take place within the huge glasshouse, but so many had arrived that it was impossible to squeeze them all in. So, it was decided to move outside, where the wide lawns could accommodate them all. Hence the unorthodox pulpit of the carriage. Moody was not one to be troubled by being unorthodox.

For five months Moody had been preaching night and day, in an enormous tent set up on Glasgow Green and in the City Halls, but now he was to move on to other towns and cities across Scotland. He hadn't really planned to spend time in Scotland at all, but while he was in the north of England a minister from Leith, the Rev John Kelman, hearing of the impact of Moody's preaching in Sunderland, travelled down to see him and to beg him to come north. There was great need, said Kelman, and he believed that Moody's message would touch the hearts and lives of countless men and women. Scotland was ripe for revival, he said. He was to be proved wonderfully right.

So, Moody came, together with his singing friend, Ira Sankey. And just as Kelman had said, they found huge numbers of very responsive people – workmen from the foundries and shipyards and coal mines, shopkeepers and housemaids, university students, businessmen and doctors, apprentices and teachers and housewives: rich and poor, and everything in between. Accustomed as many of them were to a rather austere model of church teaching, often focusing on the judgment of God, and to preaching too learned for the uneducated, Moody's persistent message of the love and grace of God, and of God's longing to welcome any who would turn to him, together with the evangelist's use of simple language and homely stories, brought the gospel alive and fresh and understandable to the listening crowds. That final night was to have repercussions not just for Scotland but soon for the wider world. Many, from all walks of life, came to personal saving faith in the Lord Jesus Christ that night, and many went on to a lifetime of witness and service. It was said that more than 3,000 dedicated their lives to the Lord

Jesus Christ over the final few days of the campaign, as well as energising already-believers to ardent evangelism. But, in addition, it was to give rise to numerous agencies, alongside the local churches, addressing specific needs, especially in the cities and among the urban poor, many of whom were by and large beyond the effective reach of the established churches. It strengthened the recent development of interdenominational service in the cause of the gospel. It was to lead to a number of initiatives, highly significant for Scotland and far beyond. It brought a burning appetite for personal and group study of God's Word, the Bible.

It was these factors that came together in 1892 in the founding of the Bible Training Institute, the BTI, modelled on the similar training Institute that Moody had set up in Chicago three years before. It is the story of the Glasgow BTI (and its later evolutions into the Glasgow Bible College, and finally the International Christian College) that is the focus of this book. It is a story to inspire and to celebrate, as God used it to shape men and women down through many years, and through them to bring the gospel far and wide. Only God himself knows how many were ushered into the Kingdom of God through them. It is not for us to try to assert numbers. It is enough to trace the hand of God's grace and blessing, and to trust him for all that he sovereignly chose to do.

But it also inspires us to believe that God is well able to do great things in difficult and complex contexts – an encouragement and a challenge for us today, in a Scotland that has once again drifted far from its Christian heritage. Spiritual revival is not simply consigned to the past, it is something for today's believers to seek and to pray for, in faith and hope.

2

Glasgow,
thriving city?

BY THE time of Moody's visit, Glasgow was a rapidly growing city, a city of contradictions, of great poverty and of great wealth, of energy and weariness. As for many British cities from the late eighteenth century onwards, the Industrial Revolution created immense opportunities for some, and gruesome toil and suffering for others. The population had mushroomed, from around 84,000 in 1801 to more than 750,000 by the mid 1870s, with all the acute problems associated with so much migration from the countryside to a city unable to absorb such growth in a healthy fashion.

While those with wealth and transport to do so moved steadily westwards, where the air was cleaner and green spaces more frequent, most of those who laboured in any of the many heavy industries found themselves increasingly crammed into old dilapidated buildings, with a family or more jammed into a single room, and with the most rudimentary sanitary arrangements. For them, a glimpse of sky or of a tree was a rare luxury, and water only to be obtained from a pump in the street or a tiny backyard. No wonder that disease was rife, and mortality rates, especially among children or for women in childbirth, were very high.

Why did people come? For some there was the usually unfulfilled hope that life could only be better in a bustling city than in an increasingly impoverished countryside. For others, the Highland Clearances had already separated them from the land from which they managed some level of subsistence, and migrate they must, and Glasgow was nearer than across the sea to Canada. Some had heard rags-to-riches stories, and gambled that they might be lucky, too. Others fled potato famines in Ireland, or the hunger from rain-ruined oat harvests in Scotland. Some came to join relatives already there. Some knew there was labour, hard and ill-paid though it might be, to be had in the shipyards and iron works, the mines and the docks and the factories, and in a world whose changes they found hard to understand, some wage was better than none.

There was a huge appetite for new ships, and for years the Clyde became the place above all where they were being built – for centuries wooden sailing ships, and then the new world of steam ships, increasingly with iron, then steel, hulls. To build such ships, you need iron and steel works, and coal to fire them up and to keep the steam flowing, you need men, thousands of them, to pour their lives into producing all the needed materials and then to fashion those materials into larger and larger ships, for trade, for leisure travel, for connecting with the wider world. And it was not only ships that were being built, but trains, too. In 1850, there were 7,000 miles of railway lines in Britain; by 1890, that had risen to 20,000 miles, and Glasgow was building railway steam engines, railway carriages, and the tracks to carry them, not only for Britain but also for the Empire. There was a bottomless pit for labourers, and indeed for some increasingly skilled men as well.

There were the students who came to study in the growing university, engineers drawn to a city with fast developing industry, entrepreneurs of many kinds eagerly looking for opportunities to be seized, architects and builders, owners of the various industries, painters and poets, and a host of others, most of these well insulated from the squalor of the poor. Alongside them were very large numbers of men and women in domestic service - housemaids, cooks, coachmen and grooms, messenger boys – and an army of shopkeepers and artisans, landlords, brewers and inn-keepers.

So, depending on whether you lived in a slum or a mansion, your view of Glasgow life, and daily experience, could vary enormously. But, if you wanted tea brought by the graceful tea clippers racing up the Clyde after their long journey from China, beautifully patterned cloth from Paisley, a new ship for business or pleasure, a train engine or railway tracks, or coal for your fireplace, Glasgow was the place to be.

No wonder Glasgow came to be known as 'the second city of the Empire'. It was.

3
What about the churches?

SCOTTISH Presbyterianism had a long and painful history of divisions and splits. It was the explosion of the Disruption in 1843 that perhaps most affected the Scottish church landscape against which Moody was to conduct his campaigns. A large number of evangelical ministers and their congregations had left the Church of Scotland to form the Free Church. Forty years later, these were still the congregations and their leaders who were both most exercised over the need to reach the largely unchurched urban poor and also committed to the preaching of the gospel as widely as possible. That included the far wider world, inspired by the stories of pioneers such as David Livingstone in Africa, William Carey and Henry Martyn in India, or Robert Morrison and James Hudson Taylor in China.

Many church leaders had some hesitations about some elements of Moody's simple preaching, and sometimes doubtful about how deep and lasting people's professions of conversion might be. But on the whole they were supportive despite the campaign not being tied to, and controlled by, a local church and its parish.

There was still a widespread assumption that God had ordained 'the rich man in his castle and the poor man at his gate' as the right arrangement for society, and the Lord's saying 'the poor you will always have with you' was often seen as justification for social stratification. That belief, however, did not mean that the poor did not need the gospel: they could, and needed to, become the righteous poor as opposed to the wicked, improvident and irreligious poor. Addressing their social and economic status was of secondary importance, except in so far as it stood in the way of their eternal and spiritual condition. If reaching them meant a simple gospel, so be it.

Such beliefs sit uneasily for us today, where commitment to the integral or holistic gospel is widely accepted among evangelicals. Indeed, there were Scots for whom it sat uneasily from well before Moody's advent. Notable among them was the Rev Thomas Chalmers, who as early as 1815 was addressing the responsibility of his Glasgow churches, one after the other, to reach far more effectively the swelling numbers of indigenous poor and poor migrants crammed into his parish. He was to go on to teach at both Glasgow and Edinburgh Universities, and to challenge the ministerial students he was helping train to ensure the churches engaged fully with social needs as well as spiritual ones. He believed the church could be a catalyst to enable even the poor to improve their own community as well as needing support from outside.

The 1843 Disruption paradoxically also gave impetus to interdenominational activity. Just because there were passionate convictions that had led to the parting of the ways, that did not mean that those from whom you separated should be condemned out of hand. The Body of Christ mattered. So, in 1846, a group of mainly Scottish church leaders came together to form the Evangelical Alliance. The aim was to foster co-operation between those equally committed to the cause of the gospel and the authority of God's Word, even though they might disagree on a number of other matters such as how a church should be organised or exactly how baptism should be administered. There were already a small handful of such arrangements, such as the establishing of Bible Societies, or the Abolition of Slavery movement spearheaded by William Wilberforce and his Clapham friends. Like-minded Christians could join together for specific purposes that transcended denominational distinctions.

So it was that when it was known that Moody was coming to Glasgow, a group of leading Christian men, both ministers and laymen, and including some influential businessmen, formed the United Evangelistic Committee to make all the practical arrangements, from the setting up of the huge tent on Glasgow Green to hiring the City Halls to procuring Bibles and Gospel portions from the Bible Society to offer to those who came to faith. They gathered together the finance needed, organised helpers such as men and women to counsel those wanting to respond to the message, and worked to encourage local church leaders to be supportive – and ready to welcome those who came to faith.

The formation of this Committee was to lead to long-term consequences.

4

The Glasgow United Evangelistic Association

BY THE conclusion of that extraordinary night in the Botanic Gardens it was absolutely clear that, under God's good hand, this was not the end but the beginning of a movement of the Holy Spirit in Glasgow.

So, what had begun as a committee for a specific and temporary purpose evolved into The Glasgow United Evangelistic Association, which was to have a long and fruitful life. It was to give rise to numerous ministries. The big tent on Glasgow Green remained for two years while a permanent building could be built, named in recognition of its origins The Tent Hall. For two years, every Sunday morning, long lines of poor or homeless or destitute men and women and children came for a free hot and filling breakfast, followed by a brief service.

Lord Overtoun: early sponsor of BTI

When the new Tent Hall was completed, the breakfasts simply relocated there, serving often two thousand or more every week with good food and loving care. Soon there were nourishing hot Sunday lunches, too, for several hundred of the most needy children. Before long, simple medical care was added, and help for prostitutes and alcoholics, literacy classes, reading rooms, and much more. Later came the Cripple League, providing help and activities to those with a variety of handicaps, long before the Welfare State came into being. There were Fresh Air Fortnights, where children in particular were taken from the pollution of the city to enjoy a holiday beside the sea each summer, often around 8,000 children each year. Mission Halls were set up in many locations, especially for those uncomfortable, or sadly even unwelcome, in the mainstream churches. Many of these activities continued right up till late in the twentieth century, supplementing state provision, and in the case of the Mission Halls still active in deprived areas of the city.

This multi-faceted range of ministries impacted the lives of thousands, especially but not exclusively among the poor. It drew in countless numbers of people from all strata of society to staff and run them, including armies of volunteers. It mobilised God's people on a scale not seen before in a city such as Glasgow. In particular it provided an outlet for practical service for the many single women who sadly did not always find such openings within the local churches, where the expectation was for women to focus on marriage, domesticity and child rearing. It is rarely acknowledged today in secular Britain how deeply social care and the fight for justice for all is rooted in the Christian tradition and practice.

But all this activity needed co-ordination and vision, and it was this that the GUEA Committee, then Council, provided. From the beginning it brought together able men with gifts, experience, and often wealth, and the time to give to a cause so dear to them. For these were men who were passionate disciples of the Lord Jesus Christ, and whose faith was the mainspring of their lives. They were mostly businessmen or church leaders. Most notable among them, and Chairman of the new Committee, was J Campbell White, later Lord Overtoun, whose energy and commitment were prodigious.

By the 1870s, Overtoun was a wealthy man, whose money mostly came from a chemical factory in Rutherglen on the south side of Glasgow which had been set up by his father and uncle. In recent years, Overtoun has often been given a bad press, initially because the Labour politician, Keir Hardie, in 1899 published a scathing pamphlet, White Slaves, condemning the conditions under which labourers at the factory worked. Undoubtedly the production of potassium dichromate was a dangerous business, and many workers suffered as a result, from deep ulcers and other severe skin conditions, some of which proved fatal over time. However, there was a great demand for this substance, used in laboratories and numerous industries, including in the manufacture of soap, and no other producers had a better record than did the Rutherglen factory, nor did anyone at the time know how to produce it more safely. From today's perspective, with all our health and safety regulations, the story is appalling. However, in the later nineteenth century almost every factory and industry, including coal mining or ship building or working with iron in the foundries, carried a high risk of disease, injury or death for many of its workers.

Clearly Overtoun worked his workforce hard, but no harder than was the norm at the time. Further, he did not use his considerable wealth to live a personally extravagant life, as did many of his contemporaries. Together with his wife, he poured money into numerous good causes. He bought and donated to the city land for several public parks. He provided baths and housing and education for his workforce and their families. He financed the building of several new churches, especially for the Free Church (who had lost access to traditional church buildings and funds at the 1843 Disruption). He invested heavily in the growing portfolio of activities developed under the GUEA umbrella, which brought aid to so many Glaswegians. He supported Free Church overseas missionaries. He contributed to the cost of several new civic buildings. He used his position, skills, money and time, unstintingly, year after year, to serve others.

5

A Bible College for Scotland

AS A RESULT of Moody's campaign, there was a growing swell of young men and women eager to be better equipped for meaningful Christian service. Many, though not all, had little formal education, as even young children often had to work in factories or elsewhere if they were to eat. Scottish churches were ahead of state compulsory provision, providing basic literacy and numeracy, usually at the hands of the minister or his wife or unmarried daughter. But even they were often unable to keep children in regular schooling beyond the age of about ten, and the Scottish Elementary School Act of 1872, which theoretically ensured all children between the ages of five and thirteen had basic education, did not always win out over the stark needs of many families. A girl might be expected to go into domestic service at that age, and a boy to a job in the mines or factory or shipyard.

There were families that were able to allow their children to have more schooling, and there were ways in which those keen to read and learn, and to go on learning, might find routes to do so. Some might even find their way to the university, but the greater majority by far would never be able to study there. In any case, if you wanted to study the Bible in particular, the Divinity School was dedicated to training men for ordained ministry in the parishes. This was not what many young converts were suited for, and women of course were totally excluded.

Moody's preaching had impacted a wide cross-section of the population, including many young people, and numerous churches had built on that, grateful to have more Sunday School teachers, or people able to do home visiting, or to help with the many practical initiatives that had sprung up. The GUEA Council were increasingly exercised as to how best to equip such folk for more effective ministry. Moody returned for shorter visits in 1882 and 1892, and the need became more pressing than ever.

Moody had faced the same issue back in America, and finally, after setting up some schools, in 1889 he and some friends had established the Chicago Bible Institute, later renamed the Moody Bible Institute. This was to provide a model for similar colleges to be established over the years in many different countries. The aim was to focus on teaching students the Bible and how to use it, on formation of Christian character, and on training in a range of practical ministry skills, especially the sharing of the gospel with those beyond the churches.

The GUEA Council were excited by this venture, but cautious. The question was, would it provide a workable model for meeting the need in Glasgow, or indeed in Scotland more widely? How might such an undertaking be financed? Who might lead it? Where should it be located? Would students enrol? The discussion rolled backwards and forwards.

Lord Overtoun in particular was very enthusiastic to see such a work started. He had been mulling over the possibility for some ten years. His late sister, Mrs Margaret Somerville, had shared that hope, and had bequeathed in her will a substantial amount of money, some £30,000, to be used for such a purpose. So, when Moody attended the AGM of the GUEA in March 1892, he urged them to start a Bible Institute in Glasgow, specifically to train people for work among those who were beyond the reach of the established churches.

The decision was taken: the Glasgow Bible Training Institute would indeed be born. By that autumn of 1892 the first students were enrolled, initially in evening classes, and so began a story that would last for more than 120 years. One by one, the questions that had exercised the Council were dealt with, and for these men there was no doubt in their minds and hearts that God had led them and graciously and gently confirmed the rightness of it all.

The GUEA had already built, and was extending, a substantial building on Bothwell Street, central Glasgow, called the Christian Institute, home to the GUEA office, and several other related enterprises. These included the Glasgow Sabbath School Union, which by 1894 linked some 10,000 Sunday School teachers and nearly 120,000 children. The Glasgow Foundry Boys Religious Society, founded in 1865 and with a membership of about 21,000 also had their co-ordinating office there. Adjacent was the soon to be opened YMCA (Young Men's Christian Association) with rooms for its many residents, large halls for meetings and regular Bible classes. The Glasgow YMCA itself had been formed from the merger in 1877, after Moody's first campaign, of the Glasgow Young Men's Union, and the Young Men's Society for Religious Improvement founded by Glasgow-born evangelist David Naismith in 1824.

Now, in faith, and largely bankrolled by Lord Overtoun and by his late sister's bequest, a large new multi-storey building was developed next door. There were over a hundred single study-bedrooms for resident students, spacious lecture halls, and small rooms for staff studies and offices, plus all the usual needs such as kitchens and bathrooms. It was a huge, bold enterprise. It was a work of faith.

This new building would not be ready till 1898: even in those days, a large, complex building took time as well as money to erect! But, by the autumn of 1892, evening classes were already being held in the name of BTI in the large halls of the Christian Institute, and hundreds of eager men and women gathered there night after night. Meanwhile, some temporary premises were hired in Blythswood Square nearby, and the first 12 resident students began their courses in January 1893.

In his meetings outside Glasgow, Moody had met John Anderson, and was much impressed by him. Anderson was an avid Bible student and teacher, had set up training classes for Christian workers in his native Ayrshire, and brought together

John Anderson, first Principal of BTI

churches and individuals from across the area to form the Ayrshire Christian Union, to encourage evangelism and greater depth of Christian discipleship. He also had a deep interest in overseas mission, and had founded the Southern Morocco Mission. He was a layman rather than an ordained minister, and as such believed passionately in the potential of precisely the kind of students it was envisaged the new college might serve. Would not such a man be an excellent Superintendent for the new Institute, Moody asked?

The Council agreed, and appointed him. John Anderson proved to be a gift of God to the new enterprise, leading the Institute faithfully and imaginatively for twenty-one years. His experience and vision were to significantly shape the fledgling BTI, so that by the time he had to retire because of poor health in 1913 the Institute was known far and wide as a superb place for excellent training, with graduates already serving in many corners of the world besides within Britain.

But to begin with, BTI launched just a few months after Moody's latest visit, first with hundreds attending evening classes, and then at the start of 1893 with 12 men as the pioneer full-time residential students. They were asked to pay £20 a year for tuition and board and lodging. For some of them, that, too, was an act of faith, at a time when that represented a year or more's income for many workers.

For students and everyone else, everything was bathed in believing prayer. God, they said, was a God who answered prayer. He had guided, he could be trusted. BTI was under way.

6

The first students

Hugh Paton   Joseph Kemp

FROM the start, under God's good hand, students were being shaped for ministries that would bless Scotland and far beyond.

Among the first students to register was Joseph Kemp. Kemp was not a Scot, but came from Hull, in the north of England, where he came to faith at the age of sixteen. He was an orphan, his parents having died while he was a child, and so was raised in the workhouse, hardly an auspicious start to his life. But now he was sponsored by a friend who saw his ministry potential, and paid his fees. This is an interesting example of how quickly news of the new BTI spread beyond Scotland. He arrived in 1892, at the age of 19, initially joining the evening classes, but by September the next year, having turned 20, and having demonstrated his ability and potential, he became a full-time residential student.

He quickly proved himself to be an able student, and gifted speaker. Superintendent John Anderson reported to the GUEA Annual General Meeting in 1895 of Kemp, …'Conduct good, a diligent student, taking a place in the front rank, and developed in a marked degree as an efficient public speaker. Gained a diploma of the first grade'.

After completing the two-year course, Kemp first became an itinerant evangelist for a year, and then for two years served with the Ayrshire Christian Union, probably recommended by Anderson, who had founded it. In 1897 he was called to the pastorate of a Baptist church in Kelso, followed 18 months later by a similar appointment in Hawick, both in the Scottish Borders.

Word of his ministry spread widely, and in 1902 he was called to be minister of Charlotte Baptist Chapel in Edinburgh. This congregation had fallen on hard times, with only about 40 active members despite 100 in nominal membership. Within six years of Kemp's arrival the membership had grown to over 600, the church was packed for Sunday services, and several hundred people turned up for at least two of the mid-week teaching meetings. Kemp was to stay at Charlotte Chapel until 1915, during which time the Chapel continued to grow in numbers and in effectiveness, moved to new spacious buildings, became a leading congregation among Scottish Baptists, and became a hub for engagement in world mission, a cause it was to follow energetically for many decades. It also became a church that sent many students to the BTI, equally for many decades, and was a great supporter of that ministry.

In 1915, Kemp was invited to become pastor of Calvary Baptist Church in New York, an invitation he accepted. He stayed there till 1920, but struggled with the rather harsh polarisation in America at the time over fundamentalism, so in that year he moved to Auckland, New Zealand. Many Scots, including some BTI graduates had emigrated to this country, carving out new lives for themselves in a land of opportunity. Following the First World War the pace of emigration to NZ increased. Soon some of the factors that had led to the formation of the BTI were being repeated in New Zealand, and in 1922 Kemp established the Bible College of New Zealand. Like its parent, BCNZ was to train hundreds of men and women for local ministry and for overseas missionary service.

Kemp died in 1933, the orphan workhouse boy whose life of discipleship following the Lord he loved was to have such wide fruitfulness.

Another of the earliest students was Hugh Paton. Paton, a butcher working in the family firm, came from West Kilbride, a few miles outside Glasgow, and in Ayrshire. Perhaps Anderson had encountered him in his own Ayrshire years. Anderson noted, 'Conduct irreproachable, steady improvement in Class work till he reached the first place, most unselfish and whole-hearted in all his work, developed unusual gifts as an evangelist'. So impressed was Anderson that he invited Paton to become his assistant for the following session. Then in 1895 he joined the Southern Morocco Mission, which Anderson had founded some years before, and worked in that country for three years, learning proficient Arabic along the way.

After that, Paton worked for four years as an evangelist, both in Scotland and in London. Many men and women came to faith through him. Then, in March 1902, he came to believe God was calling him to Australia. For three years he served as an evangelist in Queensland, where there were already many Scottish immigrants building the railways, mining, in agriculture and in a host of other occupations. A few Presbyterian ministers had emigrated as well, to minister to the souls of their countrymen, and they soon came to value Paton's evangelistic effectiveness as people came to faith and found their way into their churches.

In 1905, Paton returned for two years to Britain, again engaging in itinerant evangelism; but the pioneering possibilities of Australia drew him back there in 1907. This time he travelled throughout Queensland, and New South Wales, and then beyond to New Zealand. Paton's travels, and the many friendships he made, were to open many doors for BTI graduates in subsequent years. Like Kemp in New Zealand, Paton also played a part in the establishment of Bible Colleges on the BTI model in Australia.

From the beginning, BTI graduates, both men and very soon women, were preparing to serve in numerous countries. The GUEA report, 'Seek and Save', in its Jubilee year in January 1899, and in relation to BTI's academic year 1897-8, said that for that year 'seven completing students have sailed for China, one to Tasmania, three are undertaking some medical training before sailing for the foreign mission field, two are applying for foreign service, seven are engaged in mission work at home, two have gone on to further study and two have gone back to business'. Of previous students, twenty-two had gone to China, five to India, 13 to Africa, one to the New Hebrides, six to British Colonies, 44 to the home mission field, including five as pastors, ten were full-time evangelists, 29 were city and Congregational missionaries, and 29 had gone back to business. In addition, some non-residential students had also gone to foreign mission fields, especially in Africa.

By all measures, that is an astonishing record for BTI's first five years. The GUEA report from the previous year included this: 'Quite recently intimation has been received of a new direction in which there is likely to be a large call for the services of our students. Urgent appeals are coming from various Colonies for earnest and well qualified young men to go out and undertake missionary and evangelistic work. Some of the Home Churches are co-operating with the Colonial Churches with a view to meeting this need, and they look to the Institute to supply the kind of men that are wanted'. BTI was already trusted, and becoming known for the quality of its graduates.

John Anderson never lost sight of the founding aims of the BTI, quoted in the 1898-99 prospectus: 'The aim of the Institute is to provide a systematic course of instruction in the knowledge and use of the English Bible, and a practical training in methods of Christian work that shall fit young men and women for more effective service in the various departments of the Lord's work they may be called to occupy, either at home or abroad'.

Nor was the syllabus lightweight. Students studied the whole text of Scripture, every book of it; principles of good interpretation and homiletics to learn how to teach it wisely and accurately; Biblical doctrine; Church History; and before long Greek and Hebrew, too. Then there was attention to ministry skills such as evangelism or counselling, together with much actual application of all this through service with a local church, or visits to the overcrowded prisons, or work with the Glasgow Medical Mission, or systematic home visitation, or open-air preaching. Anderson did not attempt to teach every part of the syllabus himself, but drew in a growing group of part-time visiting lecturers, themselves fully engaged in ministry, and some of them academically distinguished. Further, Anderson was deeply committed to the development of Christian character in his students, and if that was unsatisfactory even the cleverest student could not be awarded his diploma. No wonder graduates were eagerly sought after, both by local churches and by the Colonial network, too.

Early duty for college students!
Boot brushing at 6.30am

By the time of the 1908-09 Annual Report was published, 775 students had passed through the Institute, 441 from Scotland, 245 from England, numerous Continentals, one from Russia, three from China, two from Turkey, one from Burma, six from Australia, three each from Canada and India. Of these, 403 had gone to 'Home Mission', i.e. within the United Kingdom, 83 had gone to China, 45 to India, 49 to Africa, 13 to South America, and numerous others to Europe, Japan, Persia, Madagascar, the New Hebrides, among others.

That same Report says: 'The distribution of students when they have completed their course is equally varied from a denominational standpoint, and is world-wide in scope. Already 775 trained workers have been sent out, and are rendering useful and acceptable service in many important spheres of labour. Those engaged in work at home are filling various positions as Missionaries, Evangelists, or Pastors. The majority of those who have gone to the Colonies will, by special arrangement with their respective churches, after undergoing further training in conjunction with their mission service, pass by ordination into the office of the ministry. In the case of those who have gone to the foreign field, it has been found that their training here has not only qualified them for efficient service, but has also given to some of them a special fitness for guiding and instructing Native Evangelists and Pastors.

The lines of study followed in the Institute have proved to be well adapted for the training of native workers; and recognising the importance of this department of service, we shall hope to give still greater prominence to it in future'.

The building in Bothwell Street was bursting at the seams, so much so that in the 1907-08 year there were 143 resident students, of whom 112 were men and 31 were women. In addition, there were 402 in evening classes held in Bothwell Street, and 205 in Extension Classes held in several towns such as Paisley and Ayr. Both the evening classes and the extension classes had proved very popular, and by then had catered for a total of 5,252 attending the former, and 2,647 for the classes outside Glasgow. Numbers fluctuated a bit from year to year, and would fall in coming years, but clearly what the BTI offered was both greatly needed and greatly appreciated.

Lord Overtoun's death in February 1908 was to present huge challenges for BTI. He had been a generous supporter from the beginning of the GUEA, under whose umbrella BTI still sat, underwriting much of the £22,000 per annum needed to finance all the various ministries it oversaw. BTI now appealed for £2,500 per annum to keep going. That sum included scholarship support for students for whom fees, though modest, were a real barrier. The loss of this income that had helped the Institute so much for so long would contribute to a drop in enrolments, even before World War 1 took its inevitable toll.

All the same, probably that somewhat anxious group of men who had first dared to set about establishing the BTI were amongst the first humbly to praise God. It was surely above and beyond what they could have expected so soon.

7

Beyond the horizon

JUNE 21, 1887: the bells of Westminster Abbey rang out joyfully for hours. A stunning procession of 47 carriages, bursting with Europe and India's royalty, dozens of relatives, many of them monarchs in their own right, and every important dignitary imaginable, all gathered in a dazzling array of jewels and fine costumes, to mark an occasion of global significance. Across Britain more than a thousand celebratory bonfires were to blaze that evening. Flags and bunting fluttered everywhere. 30,000 children in Hyde Park, in the centre of London, scoffed buns and drank tumblers of milk under the benign eyes of an army of well-heeled volunteers. Even nearly 500 miles away in Glasgow, it would have been impossible to miss the excitement, with numerous events taking place, and those flags decorating every possible building and lamp-post.

At the centre of it all was the diminutive (though portly) figure of Queen Victoria. She had come to the British throne as a mere slip of a girl, in a vastly different world, and was now fifty years later celebrating her Golden Jubilee. During her reign, what often began as independent trading interests, controlled by trading companies outside state direction, and usually pioneered by maritime adventurers, morphed into an Empire stretching from Canada in the West to Australia and New Zealand in the East. Perhaps as many as a quarter of the world's population, and a quarter of the earth's land-mass, were caught up in this network. Imperialism is always highly ambiguous, and there would have been plenty of people in those distant countries, as well as some Britons, who raged against it. But equally there were many who were happy to show allegiance to the British Crown, aware of gains as well as losses under its aegis. Whatever your personal experience, it was not difficult to acknowledge the extraordinary longevity of Queen Victoria.

This occasion was to be even further reinforced ten years later for Victoria's Diamond Jubilee. Few monarchs anywhere had reigned so long. These two Jubilees fed into, and were fed by, a growing sense of the God-given nature of British rule. The BTI community could not help being affected by the prevailing confidence as newsboys every day shouted headlines about India or Canada or Southern Africa. China, too figured loud in the news, though it was not of course part of the British Empire – though that Empire's military might had forcibly opened up inland China to western trade. Surely, many thought, these political developments were, under God, the way in which the Christian gospel could travel all round the world, and usher in the Kingdom of God on earth?

One of the consequences of all this was that the whole world was constantly within the concern and prayers of Christian men and women such as BTI's students. From today's perspective we might think they did not have a clear enough grasp of the difference between British culture and the gospel, and exactly what it was that the Great Commission bade them take far and wide. We might also be keenly aware of the problems when the spiritual nature of God's Kingdom becomes too intertwined with political power. However that may be, it meant that BTI students regarded missionary service overseas as natural a calling as ministry to the gospel-needy of Britain. Such a conviction permeated the Keswick Convention, too, which had started in 1875 in the English Lake District, the year after Moody's famous first period in Glasgow. As Christians became eager to have a deeper experience of the Spirit of God and a deeper form of discipleship, it was a natural outcome that many, both men and women, would sense a calling to the great world beyond, to which access was growing all the time. Soon after BTI's opening, study at the Institute in preparation for the mission field was an obvious step on the way.

Moreover, the evangelical community had a solid commitment to the authority of the Scriptures and the centrality of the saving work of Christ on the Cross. Christ alone could save fallen men and women – and all were by nature sinners and needing that salvation. No other religion, no other route, could achieve what only came through repentance and faith in the Lord Jesus. Therefore, it was imperative that everyone, everywhere, should hear the gospel of grace of the one and only true God. The religions followed by people in other parts of the world might be the religions passed down for centuries but they were illusions, superstitions, shackles that Satan used to bind them.

So, it was no surprise to have former students writing in with news in 1904 such as these extracts: from Canada, 'Two months ago I opened a new station, twelve miles from the schoolhouse in which I hold services at 2.30. The first evening I was there an old man came up after the service and grasping me by the hand, said "Well, Sir, for years I have looked and longed for the preaching of the Gospel here, and now I am satisfied"'; from Old Calabar, 'At three of our stations on the Cross River, there is an awakening among the respective tribes, the Efik, Ibibis, and Ibo'; from South Africa, 'The Cape Government kindly grant the use of a coach for mission work amongst their employees along the line. Travelling in this coach I have visited most of the stations between Cape Town and Mafeking. At many of these places my visit has afforded the first opportunity for over three years of hearing the Gospel. On leaving the station, the remark generally is "Try to come again soon, won't you?"'; or from Brazil, 'A few weeks ago, the first Evangelical Conference ever held in San Paulo was convened and attended by 50 ministers of the Gospel. An Evangelical Alliance was formed, and much blessing is expected'.

Armed with such convictions, in the name of the Living God and empowered by the Spirit, men and women gave themselves to earnest ministry. Not for them the growing claims of some scientists and those captivated by Charles Darwin's theories of evolution, which seemed to question God's role in Creation, denied

Women students, session 1911-12

Men students session 1911-12

the possibility of miracles, gave rise to the desire to see Christ as no more than a good man and a helpful example. There were undoubtedly people in the churches, and even ministers, who embraced such ideas. It was fine to take 'civilisation' to 'the heathen', they said, but not to press them to become Christians. The BTI stood firmly against such ideas.

World War I, begun in 1914 and lasting more than four weary and blood-filled years, hastened the loss of faith of many, not just in Britain but also in Europe and beyond. By its end, many of those who had ridden proudly in Queen Victoria's Golden Jubilee procession were either dead or deposed from their thrones. While the Colonies remained attached one way or another to Britain, and would do so for another two generations, the idea of Empire was tarnished, and the seeds of its demise were already sown. The Russian Revolution of 1917, the Easter Uprising in Ireland, and the world-sweeping pandemic of Spanish flu immediately after war ended, all contributed to the sense, indeed the reality, that old certainties no longer held.

By the time BTI reached its own Silver Jubilee in 1918, the world was a far different place from what it had been 25 years earlier. But, gospel seeds had been scattered widely, and in due time there would be a great harvest beyond the traditional bounds of Christendom. BTI graduates were a significant part of that story.

NATIONALITIES, CHURCH CONNEXION, AND DISTRIBUTION OF RESIDENT STUDENTS, WHO HAVE PASSED THROUGH THE INSTITUTE TILL JUNE, 1916.

Countries.		Church Connexion.		Destination.	
Scotland,	546	Church of Scotland,	77	Home,	501
England & Wales,	369	United Free		Colonies,	189
Ireland,	41	Church,	306	China,	98
Australia,	7	Baptist Church,	237	India,	57
Canada,	7	Wesleyan		South America,	22
India,	4	Churches,	75	Africa,	84
Burmah,	1	Church of England,	74	United States,	9
Russia,	3	Congregational,	71	Sweden,	4
Germany,	17	Undenominational,	55	Norway,	1
Sweden,	6	English		Russia,	3
Norway,	4	Presbyterian,	28	Italy,	3
Denmark,	1	Canadian		Germany,	4
Holland,	1	Presbyterian,	3	Japan,	2
France,	3	Brethren,	23	Persia,	1
Switzerland,	5	Lutheran,	15	Syria,	1
Italy,	2	Moravian,	7	Turkey,	4
Hungary,	1	Church of Ireland,	7	France,	6
Roumania,	1	O. Secession and		Switzerland,	6
Bohemia,	1	R.P.,	6	Spain,	2
Turkey,	4	Church of Sweden,	6	Egypt,	5
Palestine,	2	Church of Norway,	3	Madagascar,	1
Persia,	1	Presbyterian,	6	New Hebrides,	1
United States,	1	Friends,	5	Jewish Work,	6
South America,	1	French Reformed,	4	Central Asia,	1
Jamaica,	1	Free Church,		West Indies,	2
Morocco,	1	Scotland,	1	Bohemia,	1
Egypt,	3	Free Church,		Roumania,	1
South Africa,	2	Switzerland,	3	Army and Navy,	26
	1040	Protestant Church			1040
		in Turkey,	1		
		Greek Church,	1		
			1040		

8
The story of Andrew Stewart

ONE of those who took full advantage of Britain's colonial links was Andrew Stewart. Though not himself a BTI graduate, he became the person through whom more than a hundred BTI men, and later women, too, were to make their way to Australia.

His family owned a woollen and tweed manufacturing business at Kelso in the Scottish Borders, with Andrew himself for many years acting as the firm's representative based in Edinburgh. He had been converted during one of D L Moody's campaigns in Scotland, and immediately had a heart for world mission, which was to last all his life. His passion and gifting soon made him a powerful lay evangelist, and in 1893, just as BTI was coming into being, that led him to join a small party of China Inland Mission workers setting out for China, as an associate rather than full member. China needed evangelists!

Andrew Stewart, through whom more than 100 men from BTI were given passage and support for three years to pioneer in Australia

From correspondence with Hudson Taylor, it seems that he soon wondered whether his contribution might be different. He wrote: 'Since coming out a thought has been running in my mind which I think it would be wrong not to put before you. Possibly you are aware that in Scotland, at present, the Devil has been raising a strong prejudice against our China Inland Mission in some circles, especially among students and other young people. I thought it might be glorifying to God to return after a time for a tour through Scotland, holding meetings in most of the principal towns, explaining the work and principles of the Mission. My position as entirely independent of the Mission funds, etc., seems to me to point to the probability of being used to stimulate interest and liberality. I believe that I could pay all expenses of such a journey.'

The context for this was that at the time there was a considerable recession in some parts of the world, including Britain. The CIM was growing rapidly, and with its principle of sharing all incoming funds equally among members, some workers were facing considerable financial difficulty as funds did not keep up with the growing number to share them, and it was also a principle of the Mission never to appeal publicly for money. People back home criticised the CIM as being irresponsible not to guarantee salaries, and for continuing to accept new workers when funds were so low. They took a dim view of the faith principle by which the CIM operated, where members agreed to look to God and accept what he provided, whether bounty or stringency.

Stewart was self-supporting as an associate rather than a full member, so was not directly affected personally. However, he pointed out that in Scotland there was additional outrage that the CIM accepted people without university degrees, which both the Church of Scotland and the Free Church required for their ministers and for their missionaries, especially if they were to be involved in church work. Surely, they said, it was all wrong to take people from the BTI, who were 'only lay' men without ordination?

Probably there was also an element of sour grapes, as both those denominations were having great difficulty at the time to recruit for their own mission boards, while a quickly growing number were joining the CIM. Among them were clerks and shop-workers, farm-workers, butchers and plumbers, housemaids and teachers, alongside the professionals and graduates.

Stewart's 'wonderings' were cut short by his becoming quite ill, and he decided to return earlier than planned to recuperate at home. A few years later he went briefly to India with the Anglo-Indian Evangelistic Society, which ministered to Scottish soldiers in the regiments there. This Society was another enterprise to which Lord Overtoun contributed funds. While there, Stewart felt God was calling him to go on to Australia. With little encouragement in Melbourne, where he had landed, he responded to a warm invitation to go to Queensland. In his element, he conducted evangelistic campaigns for several months, becoming increasingly convinced of the needs and opportunities for many more workers there.

What was needed most of all, he believed, was a small army of lay evangelists, tough enough and willing to reach out into the areas far beyond Brisbane where pioneer explorers, gold diggers, and many Scottish railway builders, were already slowly making their way.

Where better to find and recruit such people than the BTI?

Within a few short months of his return to Scotland, Stewart married a New Zealand-born lady who shared his vision, found six BTI men willing to embark on this adventure, and set sail once more for Queensland. Initially, Stewart's father paid the passages of these men, and their remittances, but soon it was son Andrew who took full responsibility for these costs. The six-week journey was not cheap, and equipping the men suitably for their challenge of mostly virgin territory was costly, too, but that was what Stewart undertook. In return, the men must

D. Hamilton   G. Kirke   D. Galloway
Former BTI students in Queensland, 1911

agree to remain single for three years so as to be free for itinerant evangelism, to undertake some ongoing studies, and to work with the embryo Home Mission. After three years, Stewart would pay their passage back to Scotland, should they choose to return, or they might decide to settle permanently.

Having settled that first group, Stewart and his wife returned to Edinburgh, and to the family firm, and from this base took responsibility for interviewing and selecting men (and later women, too). BTI remained the most fruitful place to find people with the gifts and character needed. They were often people who were accustomed to living very frugally and with few comforts, so that pioneering conditions were less of a challenge than for those raised in wealth and ease. Over the coming years, from the 1900s to the late 1920s, with a handful after that, Stewart was responsible for recruiting well over a hundred men for Queensland alone, with others for Western Australia and South Australia. By far the greater majority of them were BTI graduates, because their training there fitted them uniquely well for the ministry to which they went, in the conditions then prevailing.

In turn, these men then largely shaped the long-term nature of the Queensland churches. Most of those who went from BTI were either Presbyterian, Baptist, or Brethren (or those simply defining themselves as 'non-denominational'), and that influenced the kind of church profile that was established, and is still evident today. By contrast, New South Wales was mostly evangelised through Anglican missions such as the Church Missionary Society, (though some BTI men did go there), and consequently it is the Anglican Church which is most dominant there today.

Stewart returned to Queensland several times over the years. He died in 1952 in Edinburgh. On his final visit, in 1938, the Home Mission Superintendent in Brisbane obtained a free Rail Pass for Stewart 'because he was responsible for bringing so many men of excellent calibre to Queensland'. Most of those 'men of excellent calibre' were BTI men. Many pioneered in the emerging towns and villages, and along the railway routes, often where ordained ministers and missionaries sent out by the Presbyterian Board would not go, or were not directed to go. In due course, many of these outreach posts, as men and women came to faith, became official congregations in their own right, usually becoming Presbyterian or Baptist. Quite a few of the BTI men, pursuing their further studies by mail combined with their itinerant ministry, went on to be ordained to serve those fledgling churches. Not a few found wives who had studied at BTI.

One way and another, the majority stayed on beyond their three years, and many settled for good. Further, they discipled a generation of Australian-born young believers in such a way that by the early 1930s the regular stream from the BTI, which had not ceased during World War I, was no longer needed in the same way, though Stewart continued to send a small trickle of workers when requested to do so.

In 1934, the retiring Home Mission Director, the Rev. William Radcliffe, wrote gratefully to Stewart: 'Thanks to you, we began to move, and when the history of the Church in the first half of this century is written, I hope the historians will have the vision to perceive that you, under God, have been its moving spirit.'

Under God's good hand the BTI was fulfilling its founding aims, and producing graduates 'of excellent calibre', and that through them the Kingdom of God was growing far and wide.

9

Beyond Empire and Colonies

FROM the start of the BTI there was a keen interest among students in the distant land of China. China of course was never part of the British Empire, but from early in the nineteenth century Britain had been increasingly entangled with China for trade. For a long time, it was the East India Company, not the British state or Crown directly, that was involved, and much of that history is rather shameful.

Britain had a large appetite for tea and silks and fine porcelain from China, and for a long time it was the East India Company that especially was the channel through which these coveted commodities might be procured. In order to pay for these things, the East India Company ruthlessly foisted large quantities of opium, grown at the time in Bengal, now Bangladesh, (which at that time was under the Company's control), on China as the currency with which to trade. As a result, unknown numbers – maybe millions, certainly many hundreds of thousands – of Chinese became deeply addicted to this foul substance. When the Chinese finally saw the utterly destructive impact of opium, they tried to demand cash currency instead, or they would stop the trade in tea and porcelain and silk. At that point, piling shame on shame, British gunships became involved to protect the trade and the British citizens involved in it. Britain still wanted those goods, and there was little cash at home to pay for it, the British coffers having been drained by the Napoleonic Wars and other expensive military campaigns. The public purse was empty. From the safety of London, opium seemed a good way to pay for what the public (or the wealthier sections of it) wanted. The gunships won, Britons could still drink their tea from delicate porcelain cups, and wear their silks, and China was deeply humiliated.

Into this context, in 1865 James Hudson Taylor founded the China Inland Mission, seeking to bless China with the gospel instead of cursing it with opium. By the time BTI began, almost thirty years later, the CIM had grown hugely, and was rather good at conveying vividly to the Christian public the needs and challenges and opportunities of service in China. This inspired much prayer and attention – and a steady flow of men and women responding.

Further, British Christians had been electrified by the group dubbed The Cambridge Seven. These were almost all Cambridge University graduates, all from highly privileged backgrounds, at least one a nationally revered cricket hero, so their names swiftly became famous. They engaged in a high-profile tour of Britain together, urging the claims of China on their audiences. They left for China together in 1885.

So, it was inevitable that BTI students felt to the full the lure of China, exotic and gospel-needy. They applied to the CIM and other bodies working in China, and by 1900 there were dozens of them serving there. Most went to remote parts of that vast country, inland, pioneering, itinerating, cudgelling brains and tongues to master Mandarin – or maybe both that and a regional language, and often encountering the simmering anger from that gunboat humiliation all those years before. The death of some of their own in China, from disease or by violence, did not deter the BTI students. On the contrary, it all the more inspired others to take their place. They kept on applying, and kept on setting their sights on China.

10

Some early China stories:
BTI's first martyr

O NE of the first cohort of students in 1893, John Young, began his course when only 19 years old. He was a tailor from Strathaven, and blossomed in the environment of BTI. In October 1896, he set sail for China as a new member of the CIM. He was assigned to Shan-si province, where he rapidly made great progress in learning Mandarin, and was quickly out and about witnessing to the Lord Jesus. The CIM had a strict system of exams in language proficiency, with six exams each becoming progressively more difficult. Young passed them all within three years, which was considered to be an unusual feat.

On April 1, 1899, Young married fellow-CIMer, Sarah Alice Troyer, who had been born in Indiana, USA, in 1871. She had left for China in January 1896, just a few months ahead of John Young. Now, together they made their home in the hills, where Young had been before. Sarah was a gifted evangelist in her own right, and had already won many friends among the Chinese women she served.

On July 5 1900, the year following their marriage, she wrote home to say all was quiet in their neighbourhood, despite the eruption of violent from the Boxer mobs on the plains below. The Boxers hated all foreigners, especially Christians, and had unleashed a murderous campaign against all they could find. The Youngs and many other CIMers were vulnerable because they were often in isolated situations and the protection the local authorities were mandated to offer was not always given.

Eleven days after Sarah's letter, she and John were both dead. Tricked by false assurances of safe conduct down to the Yellow River, from where, it was claimed, a boat would take them to safety in a secure city, the Youngs, together with a couple with a young child, and two single ladies, were all murdered. A Chinese servant, also a believer, who refused to recant, was killed alongside them.

BTI had its first martyr. It would not be the last.

The Boxer Rebellion was to claim many lives before it was ended, including 189 Protestant missionaries and many of their children, and more than two thousand Chinese Christians. As news trickled through to the students in their safe Glasgow lecture hall, it was a stark reminder to them that serving the Lord Jesus Christ could cost them their lives. The gospel is indeed a matter of life and death, in more ways than one: for evangelist and recipient alike, and for time and eternity. That had been the experience of the very first generation of believers, and of countless men and women down through the centuries. So, at BTI, as they followed the news and prayed in response, rather than deterring students from applying to serve in China, the numbers dedicated to serve there increased steadily. So much so, that by 1909, out of the 775 residential students who had studied at the BTI up till then, 83 had gone there. By the time China closed to foreign missionaries in 1950-51, BTI had seen several hundred of its graduates make their way there. They contributed significantly to the resilience and spirituality of the Chinese Church, so that despite the horrors of the Cultural Revolution under Mao and the attempts by Communism to destroy it utterly, it was to emerge and grow hugely later in the century. God's timetable is often long-term.

Reunion of former BTI graduates in Shanghai, September 1900, during the Boxer anti-foreigner uprising in China

11

A Chinese translator

TWO students of special significance in relation to China were a native Chinese, Cheng Jingyi, and a Canadian, Jessie McDonald.

Cheng had come to faith in Christ during a revival campaign in 1898 in Tianjin when he was seventeen. The meetings had been facilitated by a missionary of the London Missionary Society. Two years later, Cheng barely escaped with his life during the Boxer Rebellion while living in Peking (Beijing). He was by then fully associated with the LMS, and in 1903 he was invited to assist the Rev. George Owen in his work to revise the Union Mandarin version of the New Testament in co-operation with the British and Foreign Bible Society. The BFBS was instrumental in producing many thousands of Bibles for China, and was keen to have a fresh and more accurate translation to serve the churches better.

Cheng Jingyi, at BTI 1906-08, was a key speaker at Edinburgh's World Missionary Conference in 1910

Owen's health faltered shortly after, and so he returned to Britain, accompanied by Cheng so that they could continue their work. By 1906 the task was completed, at which point Cheng enrolled at the BTI. He took the full two-year course, becoming a much-loved student by all accounts, before returning to China in 1908, where he became assistant pastor to an LMS missionary in Peking. He would be ordained in 1910. Partly because of his fluency in English, and partly in recognition of his fine character and effective ministry, in 1910 he was chosen to be one of the three Chinese delegates to the World Missionary Conference being held in Edinburgh. This gathering had been preceded by a couple of years of research into ten topics relating to world mission as it was understood and practised at the time, each topic being studied by its own Commission, whose members were drawn from around the world. Almost all were missionary practitioners (or home side personnel supporting them) rather than specifically church or denominational leaders. With few exceptions, every single one in the great Assembly Hall was a western male: out of 1,215 official delegates, only nineteen were from the non-western world.

At 29, Cheng was probably the youngest there, as well as among this very small minority of non-westerners. It is all the more remarkable, then, that he spoke twice, and each time with enormous impact. On the first occasion he passionately asked the missionary community to hand over leadership and control of Chinese churches to national leaders and their congregations. It was easy to pay lip-service to the principles spelled out by Henry Venn long before, that churches needed to be self-supporting, self-governing, and self-propagating, but too many missions and missionaries had in practice not achieved that. It was a particularly acute problem for those denominational mission boards, still controlled and directed by their western central organisation, and who therefore required conformity to the denomination. Whatever may have been appropriate in initial pioneering times, now it was urgent to hand over leadership to Chinese, Cheng said, and to let them have the freedom to develop more appropriately to the Chinese context.

Cheng's second contribution, limited like all speeches to a mere seven minutes, was to reverberate down through many years. He pleaded that Protestants should abandon all denominationalism, and form one united Church. The Chinese, he said, had no interest in denominational arguments and distinctions, which only led to division and confusion, sometimes even ungodly rivalry. The Chinese mind wanted all Christians to come together in one united body. He cited the Keswick Convention motto, 'All One in Christ Jesus', and the way that movement brought believers of many backgrounds into harmony with one another. Almost certainly his experience at BTI of students drawn from different denominations and forming a harmonious community, had been formative, too. Also, he was well aware that the LMS, with which he was serving, had interdenominational roots, though in a limited way. Further, the searing experience of the Boxer Rebellion had clearly demonstrated that in the face of persecution, the Chinese churches needed desperately to be united and to stand together in close harmony.

Predictably, there were some for whom such an idea was naïve and unworkable, but for others it raised hugely important issues. The Lord Jesus himself had prayed that his disciples might 'be one': what exactly did that mean in practice? It is a question that still taxes believers today. Ironically, it was to be Communism more than forty years later that was to force all state-recognised churches in China to come under one umbrella; all other congregations became part of the underground church, with its considerable strength, but also some weaknesses and often much vulnerability.

Cheng made such an impression that he was appointed to the Continuation Committee, which was a thirty-five strong body tasked with taking forward the many decisions and recommendations of the Conference. This body in 1921 became the International Missionary Council, which in turn would lead to the World Council of Churches, and the ecumenical movement. The WCC has for understandable reasons often been accused by evangelicals of being theologically adrift from Biblical roots, and probably Cheng was indeed rather naïve as some accused him to be; certainly, he would have been saddened by some of the later developments within the WCC. However, Cheng himself, till his death in 1939, remained a committed evangelist and Bible teacher. In pursuit of breaking down denominational barriers, he served as leader of the National Christian Council, and in 1934 became general Secretary of the Church of Christ in China, which brought together sixteen Presbyterian, Congregational and Baptist groups.

Clearly the principles that Cheng shared so eloquently at Edinburgh, reinforced in some ways by his two years studying at BTI, were principles he held dear till the end of his life.

12

Another tale from China:
Dr Jessie McDonald

THE story of Jessie McDonald is inspiring for today just as much as in the past.

She was born at Vancouver, Canada, in 1888, into a deeply Christian family. At the time there were many Chinese immigrants coming to make their home there, and Jessie's mother started to teach them English, through a programme based in the family's local church. By the time Jessie was seven she begged to be able to join in, and began to teach English to a man whom she soon discovered had never heard of Jesus and knew nothing of the gospel. She was so dismayed that she decided, young as she was, that one day she would go to China to 'tell them about Jesus'.

She heard a furloughing missionary speak about the great need for doctors in China, and determined to train in medicine. She began medical studies at the University of Toronto in 1905, one of only five women students among more than 350. It was still very difficult indeed for a woman to be accepted as a doctor, and those early pioneers had to be very committed indeed. After completing the course, she sailed for London to train in surgery (even more unheard of for a woman) and in tropical medicine. She was still not at the end of her studies: she went on to BTI, because she knew she needed the training offered there if she was to become an effective witness to the gospel in a culture so different from her own.

In 1913, still only aged 26 despite all those years of training behind her, she sailed for China, becoming the CIM's first woman surgeon. She was assigned to the CIM's hospital in Kaifeng, Honan (now Henan), under the direction at that time of Dr Whitefield Guinness. She was to stay there till the Japanese invasion in 1939 forced her to evacuate and travel west to Tali (now Dali), where she continued her work till finally ousted by the Communists in 1952, just shy of 40 years in China.

As soon as she arrived in Kaifeng it was clear that there were urgent needs for a woman surgeon to specially address the problems of women patients. Male doctors had done their best, but culturally it was largely unacceptable for a woman to be treated by a man, and consequently the majority of sick women simply did not get medical help. Jessie was nothing if not incredibly energetic and determined, and seeing the barriers to proper care set about raising funds to finance the building of a dedicated women's hospital, established alongside the existing one for men. She also saw the need to train Chinese women as nurses, and developed a training school to do just that.

By 1917, the new hospital had cared for 698 women patients, many of them in desperate need of surgery. There was civil war raging round about, and in 1917 harvests were devastated by floods. People were hungry, to the point of many dying of starvation. It was a hard year. Rampant scarlet fever and diphtheria added to the pressure. Jessie not only led the team in the women's hospital, and performed all the surgery there, she also when needed helped with surgery for Chinese men being brought in with severe injuries from the fighting. She neither ran away nor gave in, she just kept going, often working incredibly long hours and under very difficult conditions.

In 1927, a military occupation necessitated the evacuation of all foreign staff and many nationals, too. Jessie spent a short time back in Canada, but as soon as possible she was back in China. For three years she and her expatriate colleagues could not return to Kaifeng, and when they did, they found that much of the hospital and its equipment had been trashed by soldiers and looters. It was heart-breaking, and a less determined woman would have called it a day. Not Jessie McDonald. Painstakingly the damage was repaired and equipment replaced. By 1930, as war still ebbed and flowed nearby, Jessie was in charge of the whole hospital complex. She was a gifted and respected administrator and manager as well as a skilled surgeon, and the team trusted her.

In 1939, Japan invaded. As China was an ally of Germany, it was not possible for Jessie as a Canadian (and therefore part of the British colonial network) to remain. Many foreign nationals were swept up into concentration camps, including a number of CIM adults, and children from the CIM school with their teachers. Some German missionaries tried to keep the Kaifeng Hospitals going, but meanwhile the CIM decided to open a new hospital at Tali, Yunnan Province, close to the Burma Road, where it seemed unlikely that the Japanese would penetrate.

So, in 1941, already in her fifties, Jessie was tasked with establishing a new hospital. She did it. It included finding the site, getting the buildings built, getting equipment (no easy job during world wartime conditions), and recruiting all the staff needed. She was still the only surgeon, and the next nearest was several days' journey away. Not content with this massive achievement, she also opened in 1948 a branch clinic, 250 km away. It was desperately needed, she said, so it must be done. It was, though soon over-run and commandeered by the Communists.

By 1952, with a very small number of exceptions, all CIM personnel had to withdraw from China, Jessie among them. She made her way to California, where her brother and his family were settled, and applied for and obtained naturalised US citizenship. She was now 64, and entitled to honourable retirement. Instead, she joined the faculty of Biola School of Missionary Medicine, where she continued serving until her death in 1980. Her new waves of students benefited greatly from her years of experience in challenging contexts, both cultural and medical. Behind all that she did, she said, was the desire that men and especially women 'would come to know Him'.

13

Back in Britain: 1900 – 1920

WHEN the old Queen Victoria died in January 1901, the majority of her subjects, in Kingdom and Empire, had never known a world without her. The Boer War was raging away in South Africa, but that was far away from the immediate concerns of most Britons, unless they happened to have kin fighting there. Few considered imperialism as morally ambiguous: after all, it was God's will that all humanity should know and worship Him, and this was how it was being achieved, wasn't it? There were those both within and beyond the churches who raised questions about whether this was quite as morally right as was claimed. Meanwhile, heroic stories found their place in the newspapers, defeats roused indignation and anger, and it was inconceivable that the mighty Empire should not prevail.

That confidence was widely mirrored in the Christian community in relation to world mission, at least among evangelicals. To many, it seemed self-evident that huge strides were being made in 'civilising the world', that Christian values must surely be embraced by more and more people everywhere, that other religions would wither and die, and soon the Lord must return. In Britain, American RA Torrey, Moody's successor at the Chicago Bible Institute, was criss-crossing the country with evangelistic campaigns (though with less response than Moody), and in 1904 Wales was set alight with the fires of Revival.

At the same time, there were unsettling signs of trouble. The Boer War in South Africa and the Boxer Rebellion in China did begin to raise uncomfortable questions about the morality of Empire, and whether the gospel should be so closely identified with western culture. Britain of course was not the only European power with an empire: Spain, Portugal, Germany, Italy, Holland and France, as well as America, all also had their empires, a fact that is often forgotten. The wars in several of these empires, not just the British Empire, raised questions about the cultures and religions of many countries where 'West and the Rest' collided. Were other religions wholly bad? The new discipline of Comparative Religion seemed to challenge previously unquestioned convictions. Was it necessary and right to displace and replace those other religions completely, a move which also broke down traditional cultures?

At the same time, some parts of the church were embracing ideas that were hostile to the concept of conversion and therefore of evangelism and mission, or, as a result of wider philosophical cross-currents, rejecting miracles and the supernatural, and reducing Christ to 'a good man, a wonderful model, but not God incarnate'. Was the Bible really the Word of God as traditionally understood, or a collection of inspiring ancient documents?

There were the rumblings of resentment in Ireland, and the start of anti-British activism there, which was still casting shadows more than a century later, right up to the present. There was the growing influence of political socialism and the demands for a completely different ordering of society. Many Christians felt these quests were just and should be supported.

The 1910 World Mission Conference in Edinburgh was largely attended by men (and a handful of women) who accepted the traditional beliefs. However, there were signs of trouble to come when the organisers had to concede that Latin America should not be regarded as a legitimate mission area, since it was largely Roman Catholic, and therefore 'evangelised' already. Similar arguments were made against inclusion of other areas or countries where either Roman Catholicism or Orthodoxy held sway. This was an argument against the need for personal conversion, as opposed to the belief that (normally) infant baptism, or living where there was a recognised territorial church (as was true for many Orthodox and Roman Catholic countries), was sufficient. Despite the Conference operating under the strapline coined by John Mott earlier, 'the evangelisation of the world in this generation', it was clear that there were different views as to the meaning of that, and as to how it should be accomplished.

Meanwhile, back in Glasgow, the shipyards and associated industries were busier than ever: the need kept growing for more warships in response to the galloping re-armament in Germany and its declared intention to build a stronger navy than Britain's and to take control of the world's oceans. The Empire, the Colonies and Dominions, were still crying out for Glasgow-built railway trains and the rails on which to run them. Glasgow was busy.

14
How did the BTI fare?

THE BTI and its students were right there in the midst of so many challenges and changes - social, industrial, political, intellectual, and towards faith and mission. Yet, in the years leading up to World War I numbers continued to rise steadily both resident students and those attending evening classes: in the 1912-13 year, there were 75 resident full-time students, and 385 in the evening classes.

When war was declared against Germany on August 4th 1914, following Germany's invasion of Belgium, many Christians regarded it as a 'just war', thought it would be soon over, and felt it to be a Christian duty to enlist. Consequently, there was a sharp drop in numbers of men students at BTI,

Rev. D.M. McIntyre, Principal
1913-1938

as some joined up while those planning to come changed course and became soldiers (most of them) or sailors instead. Overseas students mostly couldn't travel to Glasgow. Where for the 1909 Session there were 69 men and 20 women enrolled (already a slight drop, reflecting difficult financial circumstances), for the start of the 1915-16 Session there were 32 men and 17 women. Of these 32 men, week by week more were being called up, so that by the end of the Session only eight remained, some of them conscientious objectors. Numbers plummeted in the evening classes, too, as did the extension evening classes that had been established in Paisley. The BTI, like many another community, gratefully received generous food parcels – tinned meat, flour, cheese, and other gifts – from overseas friends, in this case from the Queensland Government. Was this in recognition of how much BTI men and women had contributed to the welfare and development of Queensland?

John Anderson, that very gifted and dedicated first Superintendent, had to step down, after 21 years, in 1913 as an increasingly sick man (he survived till December 1926, dying in South Africa where he had gone to live in a warmer climate). He had undoubtedly, under God, been hugely significant in shaping the BTI in its most formative years. In 1896, a schoolmaster, James Arthur, had been

47

appointed as Anderson's Assistant, and he provided wise continuity right through till his death in 1938; but it was still a big change for the Institute to lose its first Principal/Superintendent, and the outbreak of war added to the upheaval.

The GUEA and the BTI Committee of Management appointed the Rev. David McIntyre to lead the Institute. McIntyre was a United Free Church minister, since 1891 serving at Finnieston Church, in succession to Andrew Bonar, whose daughter McIntyre had married. He was to lead the BTI from 1913, on the eve of war, through to 1938 on the eve of another war.

Both David McIntyre and James Arthur were able teachers, and took many classes and courses between them. Anderson had brought in a wide number of visiting lecturers, some of them coming on a weekly basis, while others taught concentrated lecture courses on a specialist subject, or came to teach one or two sessions. Many of these visiting lecturers were of high academic standard, some of them teaching in the Scottish Universities, and all of them godly men with practical ministry experience alongside their learning.

In addition, there was an extraordinarily impressive Council of Reference. By 1908, this numbered 68 men, many of them known nationally, and based all over Great Britain. While about half were living in Scotland, there were 11 in London, six in Manchester, six in Ireland, and ten from a variety of English cities. They represented an astonishing range of denominations, vocations, and experience, but all were committed to all that the BTI stood for and wanted to see it thrive. Some supported financially, for instance by sponsoring a particular student. All of them spoke and wrote warmly about the Institute, and added to its reputation for trustworthiness and effectiveness, and for being a good place to go to prepare for ministry. They were a very good means of publicity!

Such a community of supporters helped the BTI navigate the problems posed by the war years, so that by 1919, a year after the Armistice, it was once more growing.

GENERAL COUNCIL OF REFERENCE

SCOTLAND.

Glasgow.

Rev. The Lord Blythswood.
Sir Archibald S. L. Campbell, Bart.
Sir Samuel Chisholm, Bart , LL.D.
Principal Sir Donald M'Alister, D.C.L., Etc.
Rev. Principal Lindsay, D.D., LL.D.
Rev. Professor Denney, D.D.
Rev. Ambrose Shepherd, D.D.
Rev. W. H. Rankine, B.D.
Rev. G. H. Morrison, D.D.

Edinburgh.

Sir Colin S. MacRae.
Sir Alex. Simpson.
Very Rev. J. C. Russell, D.D.
Rev. Principal Alex. Whyte, D.D.
Rev. George Wilson, D.D.
Sir David Paulin.
F. Brown Douglas, Esq.
John Cowan, Esq., D L.

Aberdeen.

Rev. Principal Iverach, D.D.
Rev. Professor Cowan, D.D.
Rev. Professor Stalker, D.D.
Adam Maitland, Esq.

Dundee.

Rev. C. M. Grant, D.D.
Bailie Martin.
Edward Shepherd, Esq.

Lord Polwarth, St. Boswells.
Rev. D. Butler, D.D., Galashiels.
Rev. J. Elder Cumming, D.D., St. Andrews.
Duncan Davidson, Esq., Inchmarlo.
Wm. C. Gray, Esq , Ayr.
Ex-Provost Logan, Troon.
David Keith Murray, Esq., Crieff.
Rev. Alex. Smellie, D.D., Carluke.
Alex. Findlay, Esq., Motherwell.

ENGLAND.

London.

Lord Kinnaird.
Rev. Archibald Fleming, D.D.
Rev. J Munro Gibson, D.D.
Rev. J. Stuart Holden, M.A.
Rev. F. S. Webster, M.A.
Albert A. Head, Esq.
Walter B. Sloan, Esq.
John Wood, Esq.
George E. Morgan, Esq.

Manchester.

Bishop Welldon.
Rev. >. F. Collier.
Rev. W. Rigby Murray.
A. T. Arthur, Esq.
James Boyd, Esq.

Liverpool.

Rev. H. W. Bainbridge.
Sir Edward Russell.
Edmund E. White, Esq., C.A.

Louis P. Nott. Esq., Bristol.
Thomas H. Bainbridge, Esq., Newcastle-on-Tyne.
Principal Edwards, Cardiff.
The Lord Bishop of Durham.
Robert Thomson, Esq., Harrogate.
Rev. George Henry Lunn, B.A., Preston.

IRELAND.

Belfast.

Sir Robert Anderson, Bart.
Right Hon. Thomas Sinclair.
Rev. David Purves, D.D.
Rev. Henry Montgomery, D.D.
Rev. John Pollock.

James D. Crosbie, Ballyheigue Castle, Ardfert.

CANADA.

Rev. John MacNeill, Toronto.

NOTE.—The Committee of Management respectfully record the loss by death of the following Members of the General Council of Reference since its formation:—The Very Rev. Principal Lang, D.D., The Very Rev. Theodore Marshall, D.D., the Rev. R. S. Duff, D.D , the Rev. Alex. MacLaren, D.D., Mr. William Sloan, Lord Ardwall, and the Rev. D. A. Rollo, B.D.

The impressive Council of Reference 1912-13 shows the esteem in which BTI was held

15
Between the two World Wars

THE First World War had a devastating effect on the British churches - and indeed far beyond. The appalling loss of life right across Europe touched nearly every family directly, and the vast number of injured men who survived with life-changing wounds, physical and mental, was a constant and unavoidable daily reminder of the enormity of those dreadful four years. In Glasgow, men without an arm or a leg, or more, or blinded, or suffering with acute shell-shock, were visible everywhere. The many compassionate ministries of the GUEA, and of numerous other organisations, too, were needed more than ever.

It shook the social order to its core. The hierarchical system that had prevailed from as far back as the distant mists of time now seemed insupportable to huge numbers of people, and any residual trust in those in authority had mostly seeped away. Too many men had lost their lives or limbs because of the outrageous ineptitude and arrogance of all too many of those in charge, be they politicians or senior military personnel. The Russian Revolution of 1917 had shown the way to radical social change, toppling church, monarchy and aristocracy. Was this the answer? Glasgow had plenty of political radicals.

The war also shook the Christian faith of countless men and women across Europe, till then the heart of Christendom. How could you come to terms with two so-called Christian nations, Britain and Germany, waging such a bestial war on each other, each calling on God to support their cause? How could you believe in a God who allowed such slaughter? How could you believe in the old so-called certainties, be they religious or social?

Across Europe, the churches did not recover from the shadows cast by World War I, and indeed they were only to be deepened further by another World War a mere 20 years later. 'The war to end all wars' had done nothing of the sort. In the long austere years that followed the war, struggling with disappointment and disillusion, more and more Scots emigrated, especially to Canada and New Zealand. Church congregations felt the loss of many members.

And yet…...! 'But God……!' At the same time as the church was being buffeted on all sides, there were still those whose faith was as strong as ever, churches and individuals who were steadfast in their commitment to the Bible and to the atoning death of the Lord Jesus Christ. The BTI had recorded at least four of their former students who had died at the Front, and others who were injured, often life-changingly, and in addition the students who came in the following years would have known personally others who had died. Some had themselves served in the Army or Navy, but survived, to become a new group of students. It added an air of seriousness and urgency.

Soon numbers at the BTI crept up again, of both men and women, extension classes and evening classes resumed, and outlets for practical experience multiplied. In 1919, correspondence courses were also made available, which served those who wished to study but who were not free to come to Glasgow. Before long, there were people taking these not only from many parts of Britain but also from overseas. The standard of teaching remained very high.

In 1924 David McIntyre was awarded an Honorary Doctorate in Divinity by Glasgow University. The annual report states, 'The Dean of the Faculty said it was the desire of the University to recognise the value of the Institution which Dr McIntyre directs and the great efficiency with which he has organised it'. It is heartening to see the respect in which both McIntyre himself and the BTI were held. McIntyre also wrote a number of mostly small books, which showed beautifully the way in which genuine scholarship and deep devotion could combine. It is sometimes charged that because evangelicals at this time did not embrace the modernist trajectory, they 'did not think'. McIntyre was a fine example of a man whose academic depth was imbued with his love of Christ, and whose love of Christ and of the Bible was deepened by his scholarship.

It is no surprise that students could speak and write of the inspiration their Principal was as they themselves sought to marry their studies with personal discipleship and daily living by faith. There were of course others beyond the BTI community who accused him of drifting in to modernism because he read widely, and quoted from, things written by those of many traditions. He was a happy student of the Catholic mystics, and argued that there were always things to learn from saints of many traditions of the past. He also recognised that there were elements of current scholarship that should not be dismissed out of hand, accepting what was valuable and in tune with Scripture while knowing when to discard ideas and claims.

He was also happy to adopt new ministries for student experience. Prison visiting, street evangelism, work with children, helping the mission halls, and more, had been part of the practical training since the beginning. When in 1927 the old Broomielaw Church in Carrick Street was decommissioned as a church, McIntyre eagerly took it over. It became an evangelistic outreach centre for the surrounding district of Anderston, and soon also included a free clinic staffed by a former BTI student, Dr Crocket. He was assisted by a succession of students who were trained nurses. Many students, especially those planning to serve overseas, went as part of their training to learn basic medical care, sharing in the work of the clinic but also equipping themselves realistically for the contexts in which they would find themselves, mostly beyond the reach of fully qualified doctors. Even those who would go on to work in city missions and similar ministries within Britain found this training hugely valuable, long before the days of the National Health Service and free medical provision. Caring for the sick, said McIntyre, had been part of Christian vocation from the start of the Church, following the example of Christ.

16
Students kept coming...

Some of the international students in 1938

FOR years students had enrolled from numerous countries besides Great Britain. In the 1929-30 session, resident students came also from Norway, Denmark, Sweden, France, Germany, Hungary, Poland, Switzerland, Czechoslovakia, and India. The following year they were joined by students from Latvia, Canada and West Africa. Some of these would have come because fellow-countrymen had studied at BTI in earlier years and recommended it, others because an expatriate – often a missionary – had studied there and urged a national friend to go there. By 1930, students had come from 32 countries besides Great Britain, and from 32 denominations and church connections. Five years later, 1,850 students had completed their courses (in addition, many also were taking evening or correspondence courses), by now from 37 countries and 33 denominations.

This extraordinary mix of nationalities and denominations made for a very rich and formative community. It was always one of the significant strengths of both BTI and later Glasgow Bible College that students learned to respect and listen to and understand brothers and sisters in Christ whose background might be very different from their own. There could be misunderstandings, and sometimes robust discussions or even heated arguments! But in general it was an important factor in helping students grasp the diversity as well as the unity of those who love God and his Word, have shared fundamental beliefs, and are committed disciples of the Lord Jesus Christ. This was the vision of the Evangelical Alliance when it was founded in 1846. It was also vital to the Keswick movement and its annual

Convention, which was both fed by and fed into the growth and profile of the Institute. In addition, a growing number of mission agencies were glad to recruit from the BTI or to send potential candidates there for training.

By 1930, 1,608 students had studied at BTI. 780 had gone to a variety of ministries within Britain, and an astonishing 828 overseas; some of the latter, of course, were returning to their own home countries, but by far the majority were engaged in cross-cultural ministry. Amongst them, 215 had gone to the Colonies, 98 to India, 193 to Africa, 125 to China, and 48 to South America.

Students still came from a range of academic backgrounds, from those with little formal education beyond compulsory schooling (at that time still only up to 14 in Britain), to graduates of prestigious universities. The curriculum remained demanding, whatever the individual's previous attainment, but also put considerable stress on training in practical ministry and on character formation and spiritual growth. (There were also some subjects that sound humorous to modern ears: 'Christian Sanity', taught by Ralph Rumney, presumably about staying mentally and physically healthy, which would go down well a century later, but under another title; and 'Preaching', taught by Prof AJ Gossip!). By all accounts, there was plenty of laughter and fun as well as so much seriousness for students.

It was not that BTI was in competition with the universities. The Report at the end of the 1932-33 session states, under 'The Aims of the Work': 'The Institute is not a rival to the Divinity Halls of the churches. It exists for the specific purpose of imparting to its students such a knowledge of the English Bible, and especially of its great evangelical doctrines, as shall make them competent and efficient missionaries and evangelists to the 'common people' who form the great bulk of the population in every land.... That these men and women are appreciated and owned in their service is proved by the gratifying testimonies to the success of their labours received from all parts of the Home, Colonial, and Foreign Mission Fields.'

There was a huge variety of practical training contexts. For example, in 1934-35, 62 residential students completed 1,600 engagements during the year. This included speaking in churches, mission halls, and to youth or women's groups, street preaching, working with the destitute and prostitutes, and work among prison inmates. The Secretary to His Majesty's Prison Commission wrote a letter of appreciation for the work done by BTI students, as happened on many occasions over the years. That summer, during the vacation, BTI students engaged in colportage, mainly in Argyllshire, Perthshire and Lanarkshire, especially visiting 'outlying crofts and farmsteads, shepherds' cots, and the lonely places on the hills.' They took 31 meetings, visited 1,188 houses, sold 363 Bibles and 955 New Testaments, and 6,779 'Gospel Literature' items were sold or given away. They certainly knew how to keep careful records! Not for these men and women a carefree summer holiday on the beach. Alongside such work, in 1935-36, Dr

James Crocket could report that the Mission Centre at Carrick Street had that year treated over 1,600 patients that session, and visited many sick patients in their homes, 'thus doing good to both body and soul'.

Former students often spoke warmly of 'the dear old BTI'. The 1933-34 Annual Report tells us that 'Interesting letters reach us constantly from former students testifying to the benefit received in their training. One, writing from Bolivia, says "I never forget my own indebtedness to the Institute, and have often thanked God for the short two years there, and for the emphasis put on the greatness of our calling, as ministers of the Word and the need for constant and hard application to reading and study if we would really fill our calling in a worthy way". Another, writing from Ethiopia, says, "I am so glad I went to BTI; the Lord has been good to me all the time there, and I am quite sure He will see me through in what He has for me in the coming days......I saw the Emperor and told him many things, for which he was glad". Another wrote from the Falkland Islands, "I often think of my time with you, and in this far-off place the memory comes back of the happy times spent at 64 Bothwell Street...... Our BTI training stands us in good stead out here."'

During these often difficult inter-war years, some very fine students trained at BTI. Among them were, as before, a number who went to serve in China. Both Arnold Lea and Henry Guinness served till the fall of China to the Communists, and then transferred first to key roles in other parts of South East Asia, before further periods of mission service back in the UK. Guinness was one of the founders of the student movement China Inter Varsity Fellowship which played a crucial role in discipling many Christian students who became church leaders and significant Christian voices in their professions in the open years before Mao came to power. Many of them were to lose their lives at the hands of the Communists, but others, often in the house churches, were vital in keeping the flame of faith alight during the darkness of the Cultural Revolution. It helped that students had been encouraged to memorise Scripture, which stood them in good stead when Bibles were destroyed by the Red Guards in the early 1950s.

Percy Moore like Guinness followed service in China with service elsewhere in Asia, while Dr Tom Murray and the Rev Gordon Aldis returned to many fruitful years back in Britain. Among the many others from this inter-war period who went to China were Dr Emil Fischbacher, who briefly but bravely pioneered in a Muslim area, and died of typhoid fever caught from a patient; and David Gustaffson, who died of cholera alongside his two missionary colleagues in 1931. Deaths in service were sadly all too common, in any number of countries. Josiah Wilding of the Evangelical Union of South America died in 1933 of malarial fever, ten years after graduating from BTI. He was noted to be 'a remarkable man and a devoted missionary, and had done a great work among the Indians of Bananal Island in the heart of Brazil'.

To some it may seem a waste of life that so many laid down their lives in overseas contexts. It is not known how many BTI former students, both men and women, were among them. But it is important to record that many of those who pioneered, under God brought the Gospel to regions and populations where it was till then unknown. Many of today's churches in the non-western world owe their roots to those who went from the BTI and from similar institutions elsewhere. It is also important to remember that, long before the discovery of penicillin and similar medicines, large numbers of people in Britain were also still succumbing to diseases that were then rampant, and many women were dying in childbirth here, too.

Not everyone died prematurely of course! Herbert Dickson, born in Port Glasgow in 1894, and the son of the founder of Shore Street Mission, studied at BTI 1920-22. He learned some First Aid as a young man working in the shipyard as a plater, then joined up in 1914 and was assigned to work alongside a surgeon. Four months after completing his BTI course, Herbie, as he was known, set off for Nigeria with the Qua Iboe Mission. Knowing of his wartime experience, one of the first things he was asked to do after arrival was to amputate a boy's leg. Herbie had assisted the surgeon in many wartime operations, but had never done them himself. He asked a young missionary nurse to help him – she was later to become his wife – did the operation, and the boy lived. Herbie said, 'I prayed!'

Herbie was involved in much of the pioneer work of the Qua Iboe Mission, and was among the first to start a work in some of northern Nigeria. He and his wife also served for many years among the Igala people in central Nigeria. In old age, whenever he would tell some hair-raising story of his experiences, he would always finish by saying, 'Who wouldn't be a missionary?!' He died in his 80s at Quarriers Homes hospital.

Another student, in this case at BTI from 1932-34, was Emmanuel Gebre Seallassie from Ethiopia, born in 1910. He returned after BTI to Addis Ababa, and taught in a mission school for boys. In January 1937, he led 'a most fruitful evangelistic campaign in town', which did not go down well with either the Italian Occupation, or with the Orthodox Church leadership. At the time there were only about 200 Ethiopians in Addis who would openly call themselves evangelicals. The following June he was arrested, and taken to the island of Denane, where he spent the next three years in an Italian concentration camp. There had been some confusion in the Italian lists of 'wanted persons' when he was first arrested, and so he had been listed as already executed. This muddle almost certainly saved his life.

After release, from 1941 to 1961 Emmanuel served as interpreter at the British Legation in Addis Ababa. In 1963 he was appointed to a full-time post as Advisor on Church and Government Affairs for a Lutheran radio station, Voice of the Gospel. This was shut down in 1977 by the repressive Derg regime when it came to power.

Emmanuel bravely served on the Board of the Ethiopian Bible Society and also helped found the YMCA in Ethiopia. He maintained that Ethiopia needed the Biblical Gospel, and it was his calling to share it, whatever the consequences. He remained steadfast till his death in 1997.

17
A change of leadership

I N early 1938, both Mr Arthur, Assistant Principal, and Dr David McIntyre, Principal, died during the academic year. They had both served with great devotion and great distinction for many years, Arthur since 1896, and McIntyre since 1913. They had been a wonderful team, and helped the Institute develop steadily in response to a changing world while never losing sight of its aims and foundations, and the unchanging nature of its Biblical and spiritual calling. The Annual Report following their deaths states: 'Mr Arthur was loved by the students, not only for his personal charm and helpfulness, but for his sane interpretation of the Bible and his evident contact with the practical problems of life'; and 'Dr McIntyre was a man greatly beloved, of gifted and saintly personality, and able exponent of Christian doctrine......Many have testified to the enriching and ennobling of their Christian character through contact with him.' Nellie Thompson, a student in the early 1930s, commented years later that it was often said of these two men that McIntyre in his lectures took you right up to heaven and Arthur made sure your feet were kept firmly on the ground.

The Council appointed Dr W.M. Christie as Interim Principal, a difficult role to assume under such circumstances. Christie was well known in the Institute, as he had been a visiting lecturer for some years. Earlier he had served as a medical missionary in the Holy Land (now Israel), and then through the Jewish Medical Mission in Glasgow. Soon it was possible to make a substantive appointment, and in September 1938 the Rev. Dr Francis Davidson began his years as Principal. He was to die 'in harness' aged 71 in 1953.

Davidson, like Christie, had been a visiting lecturer at BTI before becoming Principal, so was already known to the students and staff. He had been born and raised in Paisley, and went on to become a minister in the United Original Secession Church, which was a small Presbyterian denomination, first in Ulster and then back in Paisley. He studied at Aberdeen University, and became a much-respected scholar and author, so much so that some years before he became Principal at BTI he had been awarded an honorary Doctorate in Divinity by Aberdeen. In the last years before his death, he became editor of The New Bible Commentary, published by Inter-Varsity Fellowship in 1953, the first copies sadly arriving on the day of his funeral. This was a prodigious work, bringing contributions from many people, and demonstrating that evangelicals were well able to hold their own in terms of thoughtful scholarship. Davidson was assisted after a while in this huge task of gathering commentaries on every book of the Bible, by Alan Stibbs and Ernest Kevan. The NBC was of immense significance and help to students and pastors, was used widely throughout the IVF world among theology students and Christian Unions, and had a particular influence on Inter-Varsity Christian Fellowship in North America, where thousands of copies were sold in a very short time.

But this was still in the future. His first year as Principal saw the BTI with a full complement of students despite the growing threat of another war with Germany. Also, evangelicalism was not quite as united as it had once been, as doctrinal squabbles and tensions led to a number of denominational fragmentations. This was reflected in the University world by the birth of the Inter Varsity Fellowship (now UCCF) as it broke away from the Student Christian Movement in 1928, over what was perceived as the latter's drift away from commitment to the authority of Scripture and especially the centrality of the Atonement. Recent years had also seen the economic stresses of the Depression, and some who wished to study at BTI simply could not afford to do so, modest though the fees were. Nonetheless, the Institute continued to attract students, both from within Great Britain and from the wider world, and was still a place where men and women from many different social, academic, and denominational backgrounds learned to respect one another.

The first year of war, 1939-40, saw the BTI 'reduced to a lesser degree than expected (in respect of) the number of students enrolled'. There were 55 residential students, 42 men and 13 women, and this included students from eight countries outside Great Britain. Winter evening classes had to close, largely because of the blackout which made night-time travel hazardous or even impossible. Instead, many of those classes morphed into Correspondence Courses, and in the lighter evenings of April to June, one evening a week was devoted to training for Sunday School teachers 'and others', with an enrolment of 121.

In that year's Annual Report, Davidson wrote: 'Among the many impulses created by the Revival of 1859, one of the most potent and far-reaching was the movement for training lay-workers for both the Home and Foreign Fields. Unlike the leaders of the Reformation in the Roman Church, the Protestant reformers and their immediate successors had tended to frown upon lay activity, and the unordained evangelist or teacher was forced to seek refuge with certain despised sects in which the light of the Spirit shone briefly. Nor did the Evangelical Revival in England issue in a utilisation of trained lay-workers on any large scale except within the Methodist bodies. The Revival of 1859, however, inaugurated a new era. First in America, then in England, missionary colleges, Bible schools, and training centres of every grade and variety came into being; and while not a few of their alumni found their way into the ranks of the ordained ministry, these institutions were specially designed to meet the needs of young men and women who were debarred from a full academic course, and who desired practical training in various forms of Evangelism and other Christian work.'

This, said Davidson, was the heritage of the BTI, and however it might develop in future, it must never lose sight of its specific role.

18

The light shines on

AMONG the early wartime cohort was Claud Trigger. Born in 1914, in Bristol, at the age of 16 he was converted through the preaching of a visiting missionary, Jack Rowlands, at Horfield Baptist Church. He soon became a gifted evangelist, and came to BTI to deepen his grasp of the Scriptures. After finishing his course in 1941, and exempt from military service, he was appointed as evangelist for the west of England for the National Young Life Campaign. He then was called as pastor of a church in Barking, Essex, where he stayed for 10 years, followed by 11 years at Lancing Tabernacle, Sussex. In 1966 he returned to Glasgow to be pastor of the Findlay Memorial Tabernacle for seven years, then back to Barking, then finally back to Lancing after retirement. In 1992, already 51 years after leaving BTI, he developed cancer of the throat and larynx, and was no longer able to preach. But not to be deterred, he was invited by the editor of 'Challenge', a Christian newspaper based in Worthing, to become the correspondence counsellor for people writing in with questions, and those asking for help, among them many in deep distress in prison or suicidal. This he continued to do for five more years, till he was 83. By all measures, a remarkable life-long ministry.

Back at BTI in 1939, very soon the Bothwell Street building was taken over by the YMCA to serve as a servicemen's residence and canteen. BTI was allowed to use a small part of the premises, which was mostly adequate, but barely so, for the diminishing number of residential students. By the 1941-42 session, there were only 25 resident students plus 8 non-resident, of whom 22 were men and 11 women. Both men and women at the time were subject to compulsory conscription, so that most would-be students were not free to come, and foreigners were not allowed or simply could not get to Britain. However, most of the male students who were able to come were from Ulster, where there was no conscription, or were conscientious objectors. It was hard to keep the Institute going. It was no longer possible either to recruit some of the part-time lecturers who had brought so much richness to the BTI in the past, other than a handful of mostly elderly men, leaving Davidson with the task of teaching an enormous range of subjects. Thankfully, he proved extraordinarily able to do so, with grace and competence.

Glasgow was badly bombed, with the Clydeside dockyards and the associated industrial areas especially targeted. Several mission halls had to close down, and the displacement of many citizens also affected church congregations. BTI students had plenty of calls on their time for help and ministry, both in the churches and also through the various social alleviation ministries with which GUEA was associated.

The war did not prevent some important developments that were to greatly serve the Gospel. Davidson was not the only evangelical scholar of growing stature. For example, the Scot FF Bruce was becoming increasingly respected in the university world. The need to link emerging biblical scholars, still committed to the inspiration and authority of the Scriptures, led to the formation of the Tyndale Fellowship under the auspices of the IVF, and in 1943, funded by the Brethren businessman John Laing, London Bible College was started. The following year, in 1944, again through the generosity of John Laing, Tyndale House was purchased in Cambridge, soon to become an internationally acknowledged centre for Biblical research. By nurturing mostly young scholars, and encouraging scholarship to the very highest level, but within the cradle of committed faith, this was to transform the profile of evangelical input into theology and Divinity departments in the universities, to provide many staff for some of the denominational ministerial training colleges, and also to contribute to a growing number of significant books published by IVF and its burgeoning Inter-Varsity Press. From the start, Davidson was closely associated with both Tyndale Fellowship and Tyndale House, giving one of the early annual public lectures, published later under the title 'Pauline Predestination'.

Glasgow may be a long way from London and Cambridge, but these developments also fed into the work of the BTI, not least to Davidson's mammoth task in preparing and editing the New Bible Commentary. He rejoiced that even during the dark and difficult years of wartime, such initiatives in the cause of the Gospel and to support training men and women in Biblical truth for effective ministry, were a sign of God's grace. They were lights in the darkness. To him, they also confirmed the value of BTI's ongoing, complementary ministry.

19

After the war

IN 1946, the YMCA vacated the parts of BTI's building that had been requisitioned during the war, but after six years of hard use by successions of servicemen of various nationalities, there was some refurbishment that needed to be done. It was hard to procure materials, and it all took time.

Even so, a handful of new students arrived for the 1946-47 session. Among them was Johanna Ruth Dobschiner, known by her family nickname of Hansie. Hansie came from Holland, where her Orthodox Jewish family had fled in 1935, to escape the rising hostility to Jews in their previous home in Germany. The Nazis invaded Holland suddenly in 1940, and soon began their murderous campaign against the sizeable Jewish population. Holland was no longer a safe haven for Jews. Hansie was only 14 at the time of the invasion, but she had two older brothers as well as her parents, and theirs had been a happy family home, quietly practising their Jewish way of life. First Hansie's brothers were taken away to a concentration camp, where they were killed. Soon, her parents also were taken, and did not survive. Through a series of what Hansie described as divine interventions, and indeed against all the odds humanly speaking, she on several occasions evaded capture and deportation, where she would have certainly died, and for some time was sheltered by very brave Dutch families in 'safe houses.'

She knew these different people were risking their own lives on her behalf. At one such house, she came across an illustrated Children's Bible, and then a full Bible in Dutch. As she read the stories of Jesus the Holy Spirit spoke deeply to her, and she became convinced that Jesus was indeed the longed-for Messiah her people had waited for and had tragically not recognised. For her, Jesus was the fulfilment of her parents' faith. She often later spoke of the overwhelming way in which God had become so real to her. Very soon after the Allies liberated Holland in 1944, Hansie was able for the first time to worship with Christians. She was baptised. As a result, those Jews who had survived turned their backs on her.

In 1946, still recovering from the terrible experiences she had passed through, but profoundly trusting the Lord, Hansie was sponsored by the Hebrew Christian Alliance to study for two years at BTI. She was still only 21, but must have brought into the BTI community a level of maturity far beyond her years. Perhaps some of the ex-servicemen and women who also soon arrived would also have been far older in many ways than their birth certificates stated. However it was, those two years gave Hansie the healing stability and community she so desperately needed, and she blossomed in faith. Afterwards, she trained as a nurse, hoping to go to serve in a Mission Hospital in the newly-created Israel. God had other plans for her, and she married Scotsman Donald Douglas, making their home in Glasgow, and raising her family there. For many years she would share her testimony at meetings and churches, encouraging prayer for Jewish people to come to recognise the Saviour as the promised Messiah. Her autobiography was published as 'Selected to Live', a fitting title for a woman who had experienced the loving protection of the Lord in such traumatic circumstances. She never lost her love for the BTI, either.

Despite the many challenges, by 1947 the Institute was more or less back to normal, apart from the impact of severe rationing, some of which would last till the mid 1950s. Foodstuffs, clothing, petrol, paper, bedding, and many basic materials, were all in seriously short supply, and even though students had to hand in their ration books, the practicalities of communal living were considerable. For many, including BTI students, the winter months especially were grey and dispiriting, and seriously cold, too: there was very little coal available to heat the place, and students wore as many layers of clothing as they could for lectures and in their study-bedrooms. That winter of 1947 was particularly harsh, with months of snow and ice. It still registers as one of the coldest on record in Britain.

Among that 1947 intake was Geoffrey Grogan. During the war, he had been a conscientious objector (though he had serious doubts about that position later), so had spent four years in the Non-Combatant Corps. Many of his colleagues there were Brethren, (many Brethren were also conscientious objectors), and through them he came to clear personal faith in November 1945. He had come from a Methodist background and had already wondered about becoming a minister in that church, but on his own admission had not till then truly understood the Gospel. He had then been encouraged by Rudolf Samuel, an Army Scripture Reader and a Messianic Jew, to study at BTI, with which he was to be associated for the rest of his life. This was to include 14 years as a lecturer, and 22 more as Principal and lecturer. Grogan soon had a deep admiration for Francis Davidson, whose lectures in Systematic Theology in particular thrilled him, and led to his own specialisation in the same subject.

Quite a few of his contemporaries had served in the Forces, and consequently were able to cope well with the often rather spartan conditions in the college. They were also more mature (and often scarred) than those fresh from school or who had in some ways been sheltered from the experiences of active service in Europe or North Africa or the Far East. At the same time, it was not always easy for such men (and some women) to adapt to the very different life of BTI, and sometimes they were keen to throw off the rigid discipline of their service years and not too enthusiastic about tumbling into BTI's. It was not an easy year.

20
Gathering pace again

BY the next year, the 1948-49 session, numbers had risen sharply to over a hundred. Some, especially those who had served in Asia or Africa, had been moved by what they saw and experienced there to want to return, not in a military capacity but as bearers of the healing Gospel. Even a handful who had been prisoners of war, in Germany or under the Japanese in Asia or at the hands of the Italians, had been touched by God to go back to the lands of their captivity, with a message of grace and reconciliation. It made for a profoundly serious cohort: serious about their studies, serious about the nature of their calling, serious about the urgent need of men and women to hear and respond to the Gospel of Jesus Christ.

At some point towards the end of his time as Principal, McIntyre had introduced a system of having a Warden in residence. This was often a recent graduate of BTI, or a close friend of the Institute, who was able to assist in the pastoral oversight of students, undertake some of the practical tasks which cropped up, and in most cases to do some lecturing. Some, such as Charles Hardiman, a Baptist minister, or George Bolster, who had served in China with the Baptist Missionary Society, already had significant ministry experience, and some stayed as warden only for one or two sessions before moving on to other ministries. This system became even more important after the War, as numbers increased and as Francis Davidson grew older.

George Bolster stayed as Warden for only one year before leaving to become Minister at Wishaw Baptist Church, but he continued to be a visiting lecturer. Geoff Grogan wrote of him: 'He was a very fine lecturer, with a deep insight into Scripture. His lectures on Isaiah, on Galatians, and on the Work of Christ left a deep impression on me. One year, his Isaiah examination paper said simply, "Set yourself four good questions on the Book of Isaiah and answer any three of them." He explained afterwards that he was wanting to test what was known, not what was not known, and that to set four good questions on this large book was itself a test of knowing it well. His Isaiah lectures were very thorough, so thorough in fact that in over 30 lectures he covered only the first 12 chapters of the book, but he was very strong on exegesis, and the material was of a very high order.' Later Bolster was to go to Australia to a University post.

Alex Somerville from Charlotte Chapel, Edinburgh, was another who became Warden. He had been training for the Baptist ministry and then for hoped-for missionary service with BMS in India (in Dacca, which is now part of Bangladesh). He had been ill, and missed his final BD exams in the University, and so came to BTI to continue preparation for those exams, and to gain some teaching experience. He lectured on other religions and philosophies, and was especially insightful on Communism, which at the time was a growing threat throughout Asia in particular as well as in some other parts of the world, including Europe. Even in Glasgow, there was an increasingly active Marxist/Communist movement, especially among workers in the heavy industries on Clydeside. Later they would be nicknamed 'the Red Clydesiders'.

After the war, there was increasing pressure to require a university qualification for many Christian ministries, a pressure that was also true for many other professions at the time, for instance teaching. That pressure was only to grow steadily in future years. The Bible Training Institute Diploma had in the past deservedly earned a good reputation for its thoroughness, content, and value, and had served very well, but Dr Davidson was far-sighted enough to know that it would be prudent to offer also courses with a university award attached. So, in 1947 he arranged permission with London University to be a recognised provider of the London University Certificate of Proficiency in Religious Knowledge (CRK). His own academic record would have been significant in securing that permission. The BTI courses were adjusted in such a way that a student could combine study for the Institute's own Diploma with the CRK. Not all students chose such a route as it did involve quite a bit of additional work, but for many students it offered the best of both worlds – all the things that BTI did best, including practical ministry and spiritual formation, with the more theoretical focus of the CRK and its recognition, for instance for teaching Religious Education in schools.

Davidson was keen to offer the BD (Bachelor of Divinity), too, for similar reasons, and arranged with London that BTI could indeed do that; but initially that was a step too far for students, and it was to be some years later before students chose to combine the BTI's own Diploma, with all its significant demands, with the BD as well. The BTI courses were rigorous and demanding in their own right, and were no lazy option. They often involved work and study quite as demanding as what was required in the universities, plus the practical ministry that the universities did not. In fact, years later, in the 1980s, a student who arrived complete with a PhD said that she had never worked so hard in her life as she found she needed to do at BTI!

The Carrick Street Mission absorbed a lot of time and effort, with compulsory attendance twice a week, on Sundays and Thursdays, unless involved in some other ministry appointment, and open-air meetings, too. The Institute was still receiving many requests for preachers and speakers at mission halls, small churches, and elsewhere, and sometimes a small team would go, to sing, and give a testimony, as well as preach. There was still follow-up visiting in homes to be done, and in the summer holiday students were expected to take part in seaside missions, or local church missions. One evening a week, there was required attendance at a missionary meeting within the College, where guest speakers came and talked about the ministry in which they were involved, and there were prayer meetings, too. Lectures were mostly crammed into a long morning, so that afternoons could be largely devoted to personal study and essay writing, with one afternoon dedicated to outside exercise – a long walk or perhaps a game of football. It was a demanding schedule; but afterwards many former students would testify that such training and discipline had stood them in good stead when they moved on into ministry.

With such a demanding life-style, there was often plenty of pastoral work for the Warden to do, encouraging the faint-hearted or struggling, chivvying the dilatory, listening to those who needed a sympathetic ear, praying for them all. By now there was also a Matron, whose responsibility was to support the female students in the same way, and also to deal with health issues among the whole community. It was usually a trained nurse who took this role, sometimes one who had missionary experience overseas as well.

21

Some early 1950s students

THE number of students coming from Europe was steadily recovering its pre- war pattern. Most remarkable of all – though entirely consistent with the reconciling nature of the Gospel – in 1952 four German students arrived. They had all been students at the Beatenburg Bible College in Switzerland, but for some reason had not settled there, and so transferred as a group to the BTI. Among them was Wolfgang Schroder. At the age of 18, he had been a civic leader in Communist East Germany, and in that role had been sent to spy on a Christian meeting. In the grace of God, what he heard there changed his life, and he had come to faith in Christ. For all four, their time at BTI proved very formative; several of them became pastors in the Lutheran Church back in Germany, another a missionary, bringing the healing message of forgiveness and new life in Christ,

Rowland Bell, pioneer church planter in Thailand

and of the family-ness of God's people, transcending past enmities. They found acceptance and welcome among the BTI community, even from those whose families had suffered greatly during the war.

Another European was Elly Van der Linden from the Netherlands. Before she was a Christian, she had been keen to learn English well, and was told by her teacher that the best way to do that was to attend an English-speaking congregation in Amsterdam, where she would get lots of conversational practice. This completely non-spiritual motive was transformed by God in his grace, and Elly came to vibrant faith in Christ. Soon she felt called to missionary service, and training at BTI looked the best possible preparation. The two years at BTI were all that she had hoped for and more, and led her on to a lifetime of service in East Asia, among the tribal Mangyan peoples of the Philippines. Her gift for languages enabled her to work among a group for whom when she arrived there was no written language, no Scriptures, and no known believers. By the time she left, there was the strong nucleus of a church, equipped leaders and indigenous pastors, a written language, and the start of translated Scriptures.

Tom Graumann was originally from Brno, Czechoslovakia. Born in 1931, he came from a Jewish family, although his parents were not practising Jews. They had plenty of money, were experienced paediatricians, and lived well, but as Hitler came to power and his threats against Jews intensified, Tom's parents decided reluctantly to take up Nicholas Winton's offer to arrange travel for him to Britain and safety. Like most families at the time, they hoped and expected the separation to be quite temporary. In fact, soon after Tom's rescue his parents were rounded up and died shortly after. Tom found himself taken in by a lady who had been a teacher in a mission school in Jaffa, Palestine, and was now unable to return. Mary Corson lived in the village of Connel Ferry, near Oban on the west coast of Scotland, and with some apprehension took in two small boys, Tom and one other. She read a passage of the Bible every day to Tom and his companion refugee, and took them to Sunday School, then a few months later to a mission to children conducted by Hudson Pope of the Children's Special Service Mission. Tom later wrote, 'I bowed my head and asked Jesus to be my Saviour'. Tragedy had become a path to faith.

Later, at BTI, Tom was especially arrested by a speaker at one of the weekly missionary meetings, who had been working in the Philippines. As a result, after BTI Tom went there, to work with a small rural church. He met and married a Canadian. After eight years, and following problems relating to adopting two babies, they went to live in North America, and worked among refugees and international students. Then in the 1990s, Tom's grandmother's home was returned to the family, and Tom and his wife decided to go back to the Czech Republic, to work among students there, to teach English, and to share their story of how God had rescued Tom from certain death and led them all the years since.

Different from these European students were Rowland and Kathie Bell. Rowland, born in 1927 in a small village in Cumbria, north-west England, had little formal education, but following his conversion in his late teens he had a passionate desire to share the gospel with whoever would listen. He arrived at BTI in 1951 (where he met Kathie) and revelled in the opportunity to study and learn, in an environment where those with limited prior education were enabled to blossom and flourish. He became an avid student, evidencing that in the right conditions lack of previous schooling need not define a person for life. For the rest of his life, Rowland never stopped studying and learning, while also deeply committed to helping others from similar backgrounds to thrive in their turn.

After BTI, he and Kathie went to Thailand, where they served for 37 years, interrupted only by occasional home leaves and one two-year period of multiple surgery in Edinburgh for cancer. He loved working with rural Thai, themselves with very limited formal education, and also training rural farmers for effective church leadership. He devised a Home Bible Seminary, enabling students across central Thailand to study while still in their home areas, with occasional short gatherings together. He wrote much of the material himself, painstakingly cranking out copies on an old roneo machine (distant forerunner of a photocopier!) and mailing them around. He clocked up thousands of miles on his motorbike, was assaulted and badly injured more than once (and his battered face was a permanent result), travelled along the muddiest of trails as well as proper roads, always looking for people with whom to share the Gospel, or believers to encourage and teach.

Even in old age, and after retirement, he was still passionate about leading people to faith in Christ.

22

The baton passes on

IF LIFE was demanding for the students, as it was, it was also hugely demanding for the Principal. Davidson and the current Warden were the only full-time lecturers, with a large number of visiting lecturers, who brought much expertise and experience but who also needed oversight and support. Until well into the 1950s, Britain was still struggling with rationing and austerity (students often sat with several layers of clothing and a coat or dressing gown on top because it was not possible to heat the building all day and rarely in the evenings), and funds to keep the Institute afloat were always of the 'just enough to see us through this week' variety. It was a heavy responsibility. Often Davidson would cry to the Lord to provide what was needed. 'Give us this day our daily bread' was a deeply meaningful daily prayer.

Rev. A. Macbeath, BTP Principal 1954-69

Inevitably, it took its toll, and early in the 1953-54 session Francis Davidson died after a brief illness. He was just 71. He was the second Principal to die in office.

The BTI Council set to work, first appointing Geoff Grogan to oversee academic work for the remainder of that session, and then looking for a successor to Davidson. In the spring of 1954, with the approval of the overarching GUEA Committee, an invitation was sent to the Rev. Andrew MacBeath, asking him to take up the post in September 1954. MacBeath, born in 1899, had grown up in Edinburgh, where his family were members of Charlotte Chapel, under the ministry of BTI former student Joseph Kemp and then Dr Graham Scroggie. These, together with his family, had nurtured in him a deep love of the Scriptures. He was an able student, and obtained a first-class honours degree in Classics at Edinburgh University, and then a first-class degree in Theology at New College, also in Edinburgh.

He served a brief pastorate in Kelso in the Scottish Borders, and then, called to overseas mission he joined the Baptist Missionary Society and sailed for what was then called the Belgian Congo. He and his wife, Emmy Fischbacher, served there for 15 years, and raised their family of four there. They longed to see revival, and prayed for years that the Lord would grant that, until their prayers were answered and they saw the awesome power of God's Spirit transforming lives. The family then moved to Cape Town, where MacBeath was pastor of the Baptist Church, through World War II and for a short while afterwards. Back in Britain, he became Secretary of the Keswick Convention, before heading to Canada to teach at the Toronto Bible College for three years. All this added up to a wide range of experience, both in local church ministry, missionary service, administration and lecturing (though he never enjoyed the administration!).

MacBeath was small in stature, and quickly became known by the students as 'the Wee Man'. MacBeath was perfectly aware of this, and was amused rather than offended by it. Geoff Grogan, who had spent two years (1949-51) at London Bible College, had been holding the Institute together since Davidson's death, and he was tall, well over six foot, and was often known as the Gentle Giant. They made a curious pair when seen together. But they had a deep respect for one another and worked very well as a team. They were in some ways very different from each other, but both, the older and the younger, were men of considerable spiritual stature, and both were loved by the students.

Andrew MacBeath was a very gifted Bible teacher, and insisted that students studied the text of Scripture deeply before turning to any commentary. The first hour each morning was given to his courses, with Grogan following on with Systematic Theology for the second hour. Two more lectures completed the morning's study, covering a wide range of subjects. Many students were still taking the London CRK exams as well, and in 1957 BTI added the London Diploma in Theology (the next step up from the Certificate level of CRK) as an option. Despite the hard work involved in combining one of these externally validated courses with the BTI's own Diploma, some 90% of those taking these options were successful in achieving their awards.

Student numbers rose steadily – by the mid 1960s, there were about 180 full-time students, as well as some evening students. Quite a number of these had been converted during one or other of the Billy Graham campaigns, 1954 and 1955 in London and Glasgow, and 1960 in Manchester. Also, from MacBeath's arrival in 1954, the growing number of missionary agencies in the UK and also Europe were sending their candidates there, appreciative of his own extensive mission experience. Wycliffe Bible Translators and the Overseas Missionary Fellowship (the 'reincarnation' of the China Inland Mission following the expulsion from China in 1951) were especially common destinations, but there were many others, too, especially the inter-denominational agencies. MacBeath himself was firmly committed to work across denominations, wherever gospel people might be found, and despite his own Baptist credentials modelled respect and love for believers wherever they came from, and displayed evangelical unity at its best.

As numbers crept up, it was necessary to appoint some more full-time staff, and as well, when no more students could be squeezed in to the BTI premises on Bothwell Street, the Institute took over two floors of the next-door YMCA hostel – a reversal of what had happened during the war. Most of the men who came had done National Service, even if they were too young to have served in the forces during the war itself, and many were ready to find a wife! BTI gained the nickname 'The Bridal Training Institute', and many a happy marriage was the outcome. This of course was not the over-riding purpose of the BTI, but was a very happy by-product. In fact, MacBeath's own daughter, Adele, living in the family home at BTI though not herself a BTI student, was to marry BTI student David Ellis.

It was not only staffing and student numbers that involved change. Andrew MacBeath's tenure began while the shadows of the war still hovered, but also social and political change brought other adjustments. Among these, practical ministry training was especially impacted: the establishment of the National Health Service meant that the medical work based at Carrick Street had to be shut down towards the end of Francis Davidson's leadership. By the time MacBeath arrived, the Carrick Street building was so longer structurally sound, and the numerous strands of non-medical work based there ground to a halt. There were still some services held, but with a diminishing number of local people, so that BTI students often outnumbered them. It was time to think again.

The Carrick Street Mission had served its purpose well, but it was now time to close it down. Attention turned to a number of housing estates – Drumchapel, Castlemilk, Easterhouse, plus the Gorbals. These were all areas of varying degrees of deprivation and of social problems, with populations mostly displaced from areas bombed during the war, with the resultant social dislocation and breakdown. They were also mostly poorly served by the churches, which struggled to establish themselves from scratch in communities that had lost their previous connections. This was despite valiant attempts by some dedicated ministers and church members. BTI students could make a real contribution, through evangelism in every form, and through helping the churches run a range of outreach and other activities. So, students were assigned to one of these areas, or chose the one they wished to go to. They were able for many years to provide invaluable help as well as themselves learning many vital lessons about work among groups who were for the most part alienated from anything Christian.

MacBeath was a gifted pastor, and spent time with every student individually. He had the God-given ability of discerning what each one needed, their strengths and weaknesses, and what needed to be addressed for spiritual growth. He never lost sight of the profound need for Christian men and women to be steadily transformed in Christ-likeness, and that character formation was even more crucial than making a success of studies. Grogan was to write, 'When a student was going through some difficult experience, he would say. "There is more to God's training programme than appears in the BTI prospectus." In similar vein he expressed the view that no two students ever had the same course.' What mattered most to him was that every student should be being shaped by God himself. He prayed constantly for every student passing through his care, and himself exemplified what he taught.

At the start of the 1957-58 session, the 'flu epidemic rife throughout the country swept through the BTI community too, leaving some 80 students ill, some severely so. Among these was a young woman, Helen Billing. She had given her testimony to the whole student body one evening, as all new students were asked to do over a number of days. The next day she was the first to succumb to flu, and within a couple of days she died. This was to have a huge impact on the whole BTI community. It underscored the urgency of the issues of eternal salvation, and that BTI was not just about 'getting a qualification'. It was about living at the deepest level 'in Christ'.

In many ways, the years of MacBeath's Principalship, especially the 1960s, were the high point of BTI's contribution to world mission. By the end of his tenure in 1969, other institutions such as All Nations were picking up the baton of preparing men and women for overseas missionary service, though BTI still had students heading there. For a long time, BTI had pretty much a monopoly in Britain for such training, but now there were other options, some of which had more attractive locations and facilities. Post-war Glasgow was struggling, its traditional heavy industries becoming more marginalised on the world stage: ship-building, for instance, was migrating to countries such as Korea, where labour was cheaper and where the industry was not plagued with strikes and shut-downs, as was sadly the story in Glasgow. It was an increasingly down-at-heel city. But, despite this, through the 1950s, and until the close of the 1960s, there was a steady flow of students highly motivated for service overseas, and MacBeath's leadership was an exact fit for the time, a gift from God.

There were many men and women whose calling was to a wide range of ministries within Britain, or, in the case of overseas students, many who returned to their own countries and made significant contributions to the cause of the Gospel there. There were large numbers of pastors, City Missioners, religious education teachers for schools, evangelists, and many another occupation. Some, especially women if they married, in the days when women were expected to be primarily home-makers, supported a spouse in their ministry, or focused on local ministry among women and children.

Since the beginning of the BTI, there had been a constant demand for former students to staff every kind of ministry within Britain. While some denominations, such as the Church of Scotland, required further training before ordaining or appointing BTI graduates, others, such as the Baptists or the independent churches, along with the Mission Halls, for a long time regarded BTI training as sufficient, and welcomed graduates with open arms. As Higher Education expanded from the 1960s onwards, requirements tended to increase for most domestic ministries, and more and more students took one of the University-accredited qualifications as well as the BTI curriculum.

There were also a growing number of students who were already married before coming to BTI, and MacBeath wisely allowed them to live elsewhere than the rather difficult Bothwell Street building. It was not an easy option as students were still required to attend evening meetings as well as daytime lectures, and to engage fully in prayer times and practical ministry. Non-resident students missed out on some of the often painful but certainly character-shaping experiences of being fully in the resident community. This tension was to continue to dog the BTI till 1980 when the college had to relocate to the corner of Great Western Road and Byres Road in the west end. By this time, only a small handful of single students wanted to live in communal flats, and after a short time these were dispensed with.

23

Some more 1950s stories

ANDREW MacBeath must have felt much encouraged by some of the students, right from his arrival. There was a crowd heading for the Far East, and some for Africa, but others were destined for years of ministry in Britain.

Among the latter was Wally Bamford, known affectionately as 'Wally from Leeds'. He had been demobilised from his National Service with the RAF, and allowed to finish three weeks early on a Friday in order to reach BTI for the new term starting on Monday, September 22 1955. Wally was a passionate and gifted evangelist, and in his element participating in, and soon leading, the three open-air meetings each week students conducted on central Glasgow streets. What today would be regarded as largely inappropriate or worse, at that time was still socially expected and acceptable, and could draw crowds. In addition, Wally led the team on early Sunday evenings to what was then known as Model Lodging Houses, and on Monday evenings helped with children's meetings, drawing in crowds of children, on the new Drumchapel estate. When did he have time to study? He must have done, because MacBeath could be quite fierce with students who neglected their studies.

Even before BTI, as a very young man, Wally had been sure his life's ministry would be in Britain. In the RAF, he spoke weekly on the RAF radio station at his camp, initiated a weekly Christian meeting, and established daily prayer among fellow believers. At BTI, he greatly treasured regular prayer with several friends in addition to the College 'official' prayer times. He believed deeply that evangelistic activity that was not soaked in prayer was a waste of time – human busyness without utter reliance on God himself to save.

Several times after BTI, Wally was invited to become pastor of a church, including some high-profile ones; but he declined every such invitation, saying that his calling was to be an evangelist, especially among children and young people, including university and college students. Together with his wife, Anne, and based in the same Mission church he had joined in 1950, over many years of itinerant evangelistic work, he saw many come to faith.

One of Wally's fellow-students was Bill Gilvear. Unlike Wally, Bill, born in 1930, came from a troubled and very poor background in Glasgow, was rarely in school, and by his early teens was part of a violent gang. His father had been converted through the ministry of the Tent Hall, and as a young child Bill had often accompanied him there before his father's death while Bill was only ten, which was when Bill 'went off the rails'. A persistent, gentle Tent Hall member invited Bill back when he was 16, and God met him tenderly and powerfully.

His life was turned around. At the time, the Tent Hall, which had come from the ministry of the GUEA at the time of the Moody campaign, was led by a group many of whom were BTI former students, among them the veteran Jock Troup.

Bill not only became deeply involved in the work of the Tent Hall, but through this also in the work of the Glasgow Medical Mission. Here he found his niche, and determined to find a way of becoming a nurse. But his lack of any proper schooling was to have long-lasting consequences. How could he possibly qualify for any such a career? National Service in the Navy helped, as he was assigned to the medical section, but he struggled endlessly with exams, and repeatedly had to re-take them. After completing his National Service, and with a nursing award finally completed, he then was dismayed to discover that his 'English qualification' was not to be recognised in Scotland. Doggedly he began all over again, with the same uphill struggle for another three years to qualify in Scotland, which he finally did. All the while, the Tent Hall leadership encouraged him.

Then, following a Billy Graham Crusade in Glasgow, Bill knew God was calling him to missionary service. So, in 1956 he entered BTI: yet more exams. Andrew MacBeath took a warm interest in this young man with his broad Glaswegian accent and vocabulary, his history of adversity and faith, and his perseverance against all the odds humanly speaking. He became a much-loved part of the BTI community, who affectionately gave him the nickname 'Gabriel' (as in the Archangel, because of Bill's smiling, shining face, and the deaf Matron's initial failure to grasp 'Gilvear'). Even MacBeath called him by that name. To everybody's amazement, not least Bill's, he completed the Diploma. It was a lovely sign that 'with God, all things are possible'.

After further studies in Belgium – French, Tropical Medicine – Bill set off for Congo, with UFM (the Unevangelised Fields Mission). More study, including several local languages, till finally Bill reached the Mission hospital in the north-east to which he was assigned. He loved his time there, and his sunny nature endeared him to fellow missionaries and Africans alike. But after only three years he was called home, where his mother was dying. In the event, she died before he could reach Glasgow; but within hours of his leaving Congo a dreadful rebellion erupted, many of his colleagues and their children were butchered, and the hospital destroyed. Had Bill still been there, he would have died.

A year later, Bill returned to Congo, despite Simba rebels still holding much of the country. He co-ordinated relief supplies, and despite great danger ministered courageously to traumatised survivors, whose homes and livelihoods had been destroyed, many also having been tortured, and almost all having lost family members. There were, mercifully, stories, too, of miraculous deliverance, and some reunions with precious African friends. But the rebellion was still in full flow, and after two years Bill was evacuated back to Scotland. After three eventful years, including further training, a very bad road accident in which he shattered his arm, surgery and recovery, plus marriage (conducted joyfully by Andrew

MacBeath) to Margaret, a fellow-member of the Tent Hall, Bill and his new wife went back yet again to Congo. A year later, health issues drove them back to Scotland, and Bill reluctantly accepted that his African days were finally over.

In the years to come, Bill was to serve in several ministries, with the Glasgow Medical Mission, the Royal Sailors' Rest, Africa Inland Mission, and finally Scripture Gift Mission. In all these contexts, Bill remained a passionate evangelist and an inspiring preacher and speaker. Even a dark period of depression, where all the past traumas caught up with him, did not mark the end. He remained closely in touch with the BTI, too, for he said that under God, Andrew MacBeath's gentle encouragement and great Bible teaching had been crucial to his perseverance through more challenges and traumas than most people ever face; Geoff Grogan had opened his mind and heart to the glory of theology; and this lad who had rarely been to school owed more than he could say to William Livingstone, a lecturer at BTI, who, realising the gaping holes in his education, had given Bill personal tuition in English grammar, writing, and study skills, every morning before lectures for two whole years. Bill's story illustrates how the Institute was shaping men and women for a lifetime of effective ministry, often through the loving care provided by staff as well as the fellowship of fellow students.

24

More stories of the 1950s
Concern for the Far East & Africa

ROM the start, BTI had strong connections with the Far East, with many early students going to China. By the 1950s, mainland China was no longer a permitted destination for Christian missionaries, and Chinese believers were having an incredibly hard time under Mao's regime. It was all the more remarkable, then, when John Fan arrived in 1957. He had made his way, on foot, through some 600 miles of turmoil and danger from his own village in China to Hong Kong, slipping across the border. Repeatedly he had experienced God's miraculous protection.

Hong Kong was still in the hands of the British, and, hearing his story, his passage to Britain was arranged. He made his way to BTI, and remained for two full years, soaking up everything that was offered, and enjoying hospitality with sympathetic Scottish families. He had a great sense of humour, and on one occasion, at a College Christmas Concert, appeared in a kilt and announced that he was no longer John Fan but Ian MacFan. After BTI, he returned to Hong Kong, worked with a Christian publisher there, and translated many books from English to Chinese.

Douglas Sadler had been born and raised in China, son of missionary parents, and had attended the CIM school at Chefoo. The staff and children there were captured by the Japanese following their invasion of China, and spent several years in an internment camp at Weihsien, along with fellow prisoner Eric Liddell, the former Olympic Scottish athlete. Eric sadly died there, but Douglas and most of the CIM children and staff survived, and at the end of the war were able to return to their home countries.

Despite this very hard experience, Douglas wanted to return to China one day. In the event, that would not prove to be possible. He arrived at BTI for the 1959-1960 session, and loved it. Communal living was not a problem for him, and he revelled especially in the practical ministry, in the Godly leadership of MacBeath, and the opportunity for in-depth study of the Scriptures. Running out of funds, he had to leave after four terms, but never forgot his debt to BTI. He left for Singapore in 1962, with OMF, studied Mandarin (with which he already had some familiarity), and was assigned to work among the Chinese in Malaysia. His experience of working with accounts before BTI meant he combined some office work for the Mission with serving in an Anglican church. He married Rosie, and together they also looked after the Mission Home in Kuala Lumpur as well as Douglas's office work and their help with the Anglican church, where in particular he became Chaplain to the Boys' Brigade.

Several years later, they went to East Malaysia and pastored the new Kuching Evangelical Church. It was a time of significant revival, and brought great blessing. Two years later, they were on the move again, this time to Miri, to pastor the new small church there and to help with the practicalities of the integration of the Borneo Evangelical Mission into OMF for that region. Then back in the UK, they served for 14 years on the OMF Home staff, with special responsibility for the north west of England and for Wales. They were based in Manchester, and as increasing numbers of Mainland Chinese were arriving to study from the 1980s onwards, in 1991 they transferred to full-time work among them. Douglas's roots in China, and their years of work in Mandarin, were to serve richly in this new phase of their lives. God has a lovely way of joining up all the dots! The Sadlers established the Chinese Church in Manchester, and soon had a congregation of about a hundred, in addition to many Bible study groups around the city. After official retirement in 2006, both Douglas and Rosie continued to share the love of God with Chinese for the rest of their lives.

A number of students from this era were medically trained, as doctors, nurses, physiotherapists, or pharmacists, for instance before reaching BTI. Many of them went on to use their skills in the countries to which they went, especially in parts of the world with little medical provision, combining medical expertise with compassionate service in Jesus' Name. For instance, Brenda Holton used her nursing experience to help set up care for leprosy patients in South Thailand, at a time when leprosy was still rife and led to families and the community as a whole banishing sufferers. The tender touch of Brenda and her colleagues as they treated leprosy ulcers, bound up wounds, and simply dignified their patients as valuable human beings, led to a number coming to faith in the Lord Jesus, and forming the first churches in the region. This did not go uncontested, as militants from another religion or simply armed robbers often threatened them or their patients. Two of Brenda's colleagues were murdered. Sometimes gospel sharing is very costly.

Others had other skills that, sometimes in unexpected ways, could shape missionary service. For instance, David Fewster had been in the family printing business before arriving at BTI in 1959. A gifted evangelist, and expecting this to be the sole focus of his ministry, he went on to Laos, working alongside Swiss Brethren, until the Communists expelled all missionaries.

Today, many Lao believers trace their story back to that ministry. After stints in Thailand and Scotland, Fewster returned to Thailand to head up a Christian publisher, producing literature in several languages, providing crucial resources for believers in a number of Asian countries. After twenty years, Fewster had trained many local believers to lead the publishing, had overseen the production of numerous books and nurtured Asian authors, and had been able to step back to support from the background. Once again, God had brought together training from before BTI and all the Bible and theological input of those two years, plus prior and subsequent experience, to create a ministry of immense value.

Ian and Sheila Finlayson were both members of Charlotte Baptist Chapel, which for many years had close connections with BTI, and which also had a strong commitment to world mission. After National Service training as a pilot with the Royal Naval Air Service, Ian headed for BTI in January 1954, while Sheila trained as a nurse and midwife. Ian then went on to Edinburgh University for a degree and teaching qualification, while Sheila went to BTI in her turn in 1956. They married in 1959. In 1965, now with three small sons, and with several years of teaching experience behind them, they went with SIM (then the Sudan Interior Mission) to Lagos, Nigeria, where Ian taught at the Titcombe College in Egbe, while Sheila served in the Egbe hospital as midwife and Clinical Instructor. Ian said, 'We covered the transitional period from when missionaries were in the majority on staff until both College and Hospital were almost entirely staffed by nationals. These were some of the happiest, and most challenging, times of our lives.'

After eight years, the Finlaysons returned to Scotland, to care for ageing parents but also because of the rapidly changing situation in Nigeria with regard to expatriate missionaries. Ian went on to teach at Penicuik High School for twenty years till retirement, while Sheila worked with 'Care for the Elderly'. They happily settled back at Charlotte Chapel, where Ian was Convenor of the Mission Committee for twenty years, and together they led SU groups and camps. This was a far cry from Nigeria, but God wove the strands together.

The FInlaysons' story illustrates a significant change that was taking place in many countries, formerly part of one European empire or another and now asserting independence. Many of those countries, thanks to missionaries and other expatriates, had now developed good education, medical and professional qualifications for a growing number of their people, and, together with a growing sense of nationalism, felt they no longer needed foreigners.

This meant that many of the traditional openings for medical or educational work in particular, both of which had been well served by generations of missionaries, were no longer available. This trend, while by no means the whole story, nor the case in every country, was to accelerate steadily during the decades ahead, perhaps especially in India and a number of African countries, but also in parts of East Asia, the Middle East and Latin America. Where resurgent Islam or Hinduism was also involved, this was doubly the case.

For BTI students, it meant that service overseas would increasingly likely be for a limited period only, before return to a different ministry in thc home countries. At the same time, more and more returnees found fresh ministry among the immigrants from the countries where they had served, a situation which was to accelerate in future decades. Keith Ranger, who studied at BTI from 1958 to 1960, after almost thirty fruitful years as a very gifted evangelist in Malaysia and Hong Kong, together with his wife, Catherine, found that ministry back in the UK among Chinese people was such a joy that he could say the Lord had 'saved the best wine until now'! Many other returnees, of course, moved into church leadership 'back home', as pastors or elders, women as well as men, or became witnesses to the gospel in numerous professions and walks of life. Their BTI training was never wasted.

25
Into the 1960s

THE 1960s were a major turning point in British culture. For the first time in decades, Britain was starting to recover economically, and while there were still many exceptions, more and more people had a better standard of living and even some cash for things beyond the absolutely essential. Partly this was because the Welfare State had now become fully established, partly it was a reflection of higher wages for many. Rationing had finally ended, more people had cars or motorbikes, there was more choice of goods streaming into the shops, and there was new housing or even new towns for many who had previously been in slums or in bombed out areas, including in Scotland. The advent of the contraceptive pill and the rising tide of youth rebellion against traditional mores led to the sexual revolution and increasing revolt against Christian teaching. The Beatles became a worldwide phenomenon, and popularised Eastern Mysticism. Atheist and secular writers became bolder, and humanist voices more strident.

It was a heady mix, and arguably brought faster social change than in any previous decade. The churches were often not very good at responding well to the situation. In fact, even some high-profile church leaders, including infamously Bishop John Robinson, author of 'Honest to God', seemed to cave in, embracing change uncritically, and many congregations started dwindling.

That was not the whole story, though. The Afro-Caribbean immigrants, starting with the Windrush generation who arrived in the 1950s, brought their own variety of Pentecostalism with them, and, sadly not always being understood or welcomed in many main-line churches, began a growing number of vibrant new churches. Their spirituality gave rise in turn to the charismatic movement, which soon leached into main-line churches, bringing new life and attention to the immediacy of the Holy Spirit and His activity in the life of every believer. It brought division, too, especially where some of those in the vanguard of the movement made sweeping claims, or seemed to put experience far above the authority of Scripture, or condemned traditional churches as being devoid of any spiritual life. It also led to an explosion of new churches, some of them led by very strong personalities who didn't necessarily want to work together with anyone else, bringing constant fragmentation. Many Scottish Presbyterian ministers reacted negatively because the emphasis on 'every member ministry' and on some parts of the experience of the Holy Spirit seemed to undermine the ministry of the Word to which they were called, and their unique place in the life of the congregation.

At the same time, there was a growing treasure trove of good Christian literature, and of high-level Biblical scholarship, too, as Tyndale House and other bodies produced excellent scholars and authors, and a new generation of fine evangelical ministers and pastors for the churches. The Keswick Convention was flourishing. And, Andrew MacBeath was a welcome speaker there. This was the backdrop against which BTI moved into the 1960s.

Despite what was going on the wider culture, the early years of the 1960s were a golden period for BTI.

It was not just that student numbers were at a peak, but also because of Andrew MacBeath's leadership. He fostered a warm family ethos for the community, in which everything was saturated in prayer, in emphasis on the Scriptures, and where academic diligence (which he insisted on) must never take priority over the need to seek godliness of character. Together with Geoff Grogan, teaching Systematic Theology, and John Balchin, teaching Principles of Hermeneutics and Biblical Exposition, MacBeath simply opened Scripture, day after day, covering the whole Bible in a two-year cycle. There were other part-time or visiting lecturers as well, and MacBeath was always more interested in the calibre of these men (and the occasional woman!) than in their official status, when it came to inviting them to teach.

David Ellis, a student from 1959-1961, and who was to capture the heart of MacBeath's daughter, Adele, commented that 'the Wee Man breathed missions through all that he said and was so often able to give examples from his own mission experience that the whole ethos of his teaching and indeed the ethos of BTI was infused with missions….We had special times of prayer for missions and particular missionaries who had left the BTI and were serving overseas; and Mr MacBeath often read excerpts from a missionary letter at the beginning of one of his lectures and turned it into prayer before getting down to the lecture'. The Ellises themselves were to go on to serve in Indonesia and Singapore before mission leadership back in Britain, interwoven with local church ministry. Undoubtedly, this missionary ethos drew many students who were expecting to serve overseas, and agencies often sent candidates to BTI for training, knowing they would be well grounded and prepared for what lay ahead. Other students were called by God to missionary service as a result of their time at BTI. Further, because of the ethos that had surrounded them, even those who moved into ministries within the UK or their own home country if they came from overseas, became stalwart praying friends for those in distant parts of the world, and advocates for global mission.

Because student numbers were so high, the BTI made an arrangement with the adjoining YMCA to use one floor of its facilities of study-bedrooms for the overflow. At the time, the YMCA was primarily a hostel for overseas students from the Universities. Friendships sprang up between the BTI men in the YMCA and the overseas students, most of whom had no prior links with the gospel. It so happened that there was a popular television programme running called 'Face to Face', in which the presenter interviewed 'eminent people' from different walks of life, and explored their life stories. Peter Lee, an enterprising BTI student living in the YMCA quarters, had the brainwave to set up a series of interviews in the Y's lounge, and called it 'Double Face to Face'. Each time, there were two interviewees, one a BTI student, often from overseas, and one from the Y, usually non-Christian, also from overseas and at the University. By drawing out their respective backgrounds and their current lives, Peter was able to ensure there was a gentle but clear testimony to the Lord Jesus each time, and a quiet explanation of what motivated Christians. It was very well attended, and led to many gospel conversations after each event. Peter went on to become Warden of a hostel for overseas students in London, and then later trained as a teacher and returned to Scotland to teach at Dollar Academy. Among Peter's fellow-students, for one year, was Os Guinness. Os' father, Henry, had been a student at BTI in the 1920s before going to China, where Os was born during the mayhem of World War 2. Os stayed at BTI only one year before transferring to London Bible College which was able to offer a full degree course, which at that time BTI could not, but BTI gave him a valuable groundwork at a time when he was trying to resolve many issues. Deeply aware that cultural changes presented fresh challenges to the churches, which he felt were often ill-prepared, and not engaging with them well, at intellectual and philosophical levels as well as spiritual levels, he applied himself to finding appropriate ways of addressing those problems. He was helped by his association with Francis Schaeffer. He became an able evangelist and apologist, especially among students and young professionals, and, now based in America, the author of many books.

Another one-year student was Elizabeth Longley, who married just before starting at BTI, and then waved her new husband off to Malaya to do his National Service. Tim was planning to apply to Missionary Aviation Fellowship, and MAF had recommended that Elizabeth would benefit from a year at BTI while he was doing his stint with the army. She was able to join him in Malaya after her year at BTI, and spent a very satisfying year teaching the Bible to local teenagers before Tim was free to continue preparation for flying. Some of those Elizabeth taught in that year stayed in touch with her for decades, and spoke of how seminal her teaching had been.

After Tim's extra training, especially learning how to land a plane in a remote place with no proper runway, they were accepted by MAF, and in 1966 they were sent to Chad, to support missionaries in isolated places or in emergencies. This was satisfying and much appreciated ministry, though difficult for Elizabeth who did not speak French. To their bewilderment, a complicated pregnancy meant having to return to the UK after just two and a half years, and then the baby's health meant they could not return. After all the years of training, what was God doing? Tim was able to transfer to developing Hovercraft for use in mission work, and this was to serve many people all over the world. Then together they were able to plant and nurture a new church in a district in Gosport where there was none. In 1994 they returned to Scotland, and found yet more new avenues for service. Their story illustrates how God lovingly brings great good out of what at the time seems a baffling setback.

26

Trusting God in times of change

NOT just personal circumstances but also political upheavals were increasingly meaning that overseas service could be brought to a sudden halt at any moment, and many BTI former students were impacted by this. Among them were Margaret Munro and Wendy Spark, who both joined the Red Sea Mission Team, Margaret in 1963 and Wendy a year later. They worked in the difficult and dangerous Afar region on the border between Ethiopia and Eritrea, in literacy and translation work. The latter was complicated by the fact that there was no word for 'faith', a reflection of an Afar or Danakil culture in which there was little trust of others. There were plenty of other cultural and linguistic difficulties, too. Bible translation is rarely a speedy process, even when there are not such fundamental challenges, and these women expected to be there for the long haul to complete the task. However, in 1975, as civil war broke out, all expatriates had to leave the country. It was to be many years before they could spend time back there, though Wendy set up Afar Aid to help a group so badly affected by war. Margaret was able after 20 years to go back for a few months at a time to help with further literacy teaching and in the distribution of Christian literature, including the New Testament, now completed in the Afar language. It was so good that Andrew MacBeath had often taught students that we walk by faith, not by sight, and that we can trust our loving Heavenly Father for His wise care even when things change in puzzling ways, and when we simply cannot see what He might be doing. This was not just for students, but for the whole life of BTI, including the staff and Council, as the Institute faced many changes, though these might be on a different scale from major political upheavals overseas.

From quite early in BTI's life, the norm for study was a two-year course, and the syllabus had been designed with that in mind. Most students had been single men or women. Now, there was a growing need for much flexibility, as students who had spent years in other education and often professional training, or in work experience, would ask to come for one year only. Some would be weary of studying, but required by a mission agency or other expected employer to do at least a year of Bible training. How best to serve them? More students were arriving already married, and sometimes only one spouse would attend; the Bothwell Street building simply was not suitable for married couples to be resident, and out of the question if the couple already had children, so more students were living elsewhere and were day students rather than residents. For some couples, one of them, usually the wife, needed to work to support them both financially, as sadly fewer churches would support a member's training. This was because British churches were too frequently losing their commitment to world mission and because university fees were now paid by the Government, it was sometimes understood rather vaguely that BTI would be free, too. It wasn't, and couldn't be.

With the huge cultural changes that were taking place in British society, coupled by the ongoing shadows of the war, more students were arriving with 'baggage' and deep wounds from their past, including more from broken homes, or from family disruption in their childhood, or bad choices before conversion. This was to accelerate hugely in the decades to come, but already required much more time spent in counselling and prayerful pastoring on the part of the staff, as well as often between students themselves. More students found the College discipline hard to accept, even though it was quite light touch, all part of the 1960s growing antipathy to authority. Some resented communal living, having grown up with greater individual freedom, though others found that very enriching.

In the past, students were strongly advised against openly courting a fellow-student while still studying, although many had happily found their life-partner among their peers, and the joke was that BTI was a bridal institute. For years, any student wishing to explore a relationship with a student of the opposite sex had to ask the Principal's permission. To modern ears this sounds rather bizarre, but at the time, a similar practice was the case elsewhere in society – in some businesses even, not to mention a curate having to seek his Bishop's permission before proposing to a girl. In spite of the rules, there were many marriages shortly after courses had been completed! There were good reasons for frowning on active courtship, not only because it could distract students from full attention to their course, but also because if a relationship broke down within the close quarters of communal living, it made things very difficult. Now more students wanted the freedom to explore relationships, get engaged or even married during their course, without involvement of anyone else.

Andrew MacBeath adapted wisely, especially when it came to welcoming engaged or married couples, while also when he felt it was needed dropping quiet words of advice or even warning. His deep love for his students, and his concern to facilitate their training in every way possible, enabled him to accept the challenge of the reality of cultural change.

27
Some more 1960s students

A MONG the 1962 intake were Peter and Cherry Brierley, intending to go overseas in missionary service. In the event, that didn't work out. God, it seemed, had other plans for them, which were to bless his people in a different way. Peter, a statistician, worked with the Cabinet Office before BTI, and afterwards did surveys for the Ministry of Defence, leaving Government service in the late 1970s to become a Director of The Bible Society. Meanwhile Cherry was a church Lady Worker, then a full-time home-maker while their four children were small. She then established a tutoring organisation which ran for almost 20 years, after which she returned to pastoral work. In the 1980s

Peter Brierley at an orphanage in Kenya

Peter started MARC Europe, which morphed into Christian Research, providing statistical information for churches and Christian agencies. For MARC that included data for much of Europe. Peter designed and administered – and published - numerous Church Censuses, which have continued till very recently, and which have been invaluable for innumerable Christian leaders. All that data has provided a fact-based account of the changes in the life of the British churches over several decades – the mix of growth and decline, the impact of immigration, new initiatives, the growth of Charismatic and Pentecostal churches, changing age patterns, and much more. At the same time, the Brierleys established a children's home, the Kisumu Children's Trust, in Kenya, which grew to care for, and provide schooling for, hundreds of children over the years. Peter also for years served as the Lausanne Associate for Church Research, helping Christian leaders around the world gather data about the state of the churches in their respective countries, and the implications of changes. Under-girding all this, testified Peter, was the biblical and theological training received at BTI. 'I still remember the fantastic Old Testament lectures John Balchin gave us at BTI, including his attempts to illustrate Zechariah's visions by running across the platform,' wrote Peter many years later. Classes might be serious but they were never dull! There was plenty of fun at the College.

Two other couples at the same time as the Brierleys were Stanley and Margaret Davies, and Cliff and Sheila Barnard. The Davies went to Kenya with the Africa

Inland Mission, and served there for 15 years in church, teaching and training ministry. After their return to the UK, Stanley became the first full-time General Secretary of the Evangelical Missionary Alliance, (now Global Connections), linking numerous agencies and organisations involved in world mission, and enabling many fruitful partnerships and collaborative initiatives. His gentle but far-sighted and firm leadership was especially significant at a time when agencies as well as denominations were proliferating, and not always naturally inclined to co-operate with one another. The Barnards went to Brazil and then Portugal, following which Cliff became Vice-Principal of Northumbria Bible College, which merged with Glasgow Bible College (the continuity of BTI) in 1998 to form International Christian College. Their ministry to international students continued well into old age.

For both these couples, as for an increasing number of BTI graduates who went overseas, their service somewhere else in the world went on to greatly enrich subsequent ministry in Britain. A year behind these couples was Elizabeth Clark, who together with a number of her more-or-less contemporaries at BTI went to India. Serving with the BMMF, now Interserve, Elizabeth first taught for 12 years at Queen Mary School in Bombay, now Mumbai. Next, she spent 11 years on the staff of the Union of Evangelical Students of India (UESI), the sister organisation to IVF/UCCF in Britain, working with students in evangelism and discipleship, and helping the movement develop a growing team of well-trained national staff, and a mature literature programme. During the period she was working with UESI, she was able to spend an academic year at Regent College, Vancouver, to obtain a Master's degree, so that when it was time for her to leave India, she returned to the UK and was appointed to lecture at Northumbria Bible College. Following the merger with Glasgow Bible College in 1998, she continued

as a part-time lecturer in the new structure, the International Christian College.

Sometimes a couple met at BTI but only overlapped by a year, waiting to get married till the second one had completed his or her course. This was the case with Bruce and Sylvia Dipple, with Bruce coming from Australia and Sylvia from the UK. After marriage, together they served on the staff of a Christian conference centre in Australia, then started two churches, both of which Bruce pastored. Then, after four years of further study for formal ordination for Bruce, they sensed God calling them to missionary service in Niger. This involved a year in France to learn French before reaching their destination in 1977. There Bruce became the Principal of the French Bible College in

Bruce Dipple

Niamey, while Sylvia used her nursing training to care for missionaries as well as students at the College. Eight years later, largely for the education of their children, they made their way back to Sydney, where Bruce headed up the Australian base of SIM, the mission with which they served, till 1997. At this point, Bruce became Director of the School of Cross-Cultural Mission at Sydney Missionary and Bible College, whose foundation decades before had been partially through another BTI graduate, and inspired by the BTI pattern. This College over many years trained numerous Australian missionaries, as well as students from other southern countries, and many pastors and lay leaders too. Bruce also became a much-loved speaker at conferences and conventions, as well as an author, and continued till ill-health led to retirement in 2009.

Gus and Eve Noble met at BTI and soon discovered they were both hoping to go to Asia with OMF. They could not get engaged until both had been accepted by the Mission (which happened in late 1962). At the time there was a ruling that engaged couples could not marry till (usually) two years after reaching Asia, in order to complete language and culture training, and make some adjustments to life in a far different setting. (This was especially important for the wife-to-be, as, before the days of contraceptives, it ensured she would be well able to be an effective missionary and competent to communicate with local people before starting a family. The ruling was dropped in 1969 under pressure from Filipino and other Asian nationals, for whom long engagements were completely alien.) It certainly gave some strong motivation to Gus and Eve to pass their language exams! They were assigned to the Philippines, where they were to serve together till 1992. They planted churches and saw them established. Gus also spent years leading and developing a Christian publisher, initially a tiny operation working from a rented garage space. He likewise worked steadily until it was firmly in the hands of Filipino nationals, with a trained strong team and their own purpose-built premises. This today involves around 50 bookstores and multiple publications.

In their final six years, Gus was Field Director, ably supported by Eve, leading and being responsible for the pastoral care of a team of about 175 missionaries. It was a hugely demanding role, against a backdrop of political upheaval and terrorist insurgency, with colleagues suffering violence, kidnap, death from cancer, and even the murder of a young mother in a robbery that went wrong. All this in the context of devastating typhoons and earthquakes, leaving large parts of the population in acute need. Gus and Eve never hid the enormous cost – physically, emotionally, spiritually – of all those years, including the pain of having to send their children away for education, but equally they never wavered in their conviction that the God who had called them was still looking after them.

Following their return to Scotland in 1992, and a period of recuperation, Gus was invited to the role of Pastoral Assistant at Charlotte Chapel in Edinburgh, a church family that had supported them, prayed for them, and cared for them all through their years overseas – and a church that had been closely linked to BTI from its beginnings.

There were many others who made their way to Asia. Among them were Alan and Maelynn Ellard, who went on to spend a lifetime in Thailand. Initially in South Thailand, a region where the majority of the population is Muslim rather than Buddhist like the rest of the country, Maelynn, as a pharmacist by training, was able to work at the small Saiburi Christian Hospital, while Alan focused on building friendships with local men and the Thai Buddhists, and the tiny emerging church. After 13 hard years, they moved up to central Thailand, where numerous small churches were slowly being established. Working with those churches was to be their ministry until 1991, when they became increasingly exercised about the need for compassionate care in the name of Christ among the growing flood of people infected with HIV, and also for the growing number of children left orphans as their parents died of AIDs. Some of those children themselves had become HIV+ and relatives and communities were fearful of having anything to do with them.

The Ellards established ACET Thailand, ACET being an international charity working among AIDs sufferers, and set up a magazine to educate Christians in particular about caring for these people, especially the children. They also visited sufferers in their homes. A Thai pastor set up an orphanage, the House of Grace, and the Ellards, teaming up with him, became deeply involved in caring for the children. With the advent of retroviral drugs, by the 1990s fewer people were dying of AIDs, but there were still large numbers of children left as orphans or whose frail parents could no longer look after them. Some of the children were themselves HIV+, others simply had no adult relative willing or able to care for them. There were often as many as 60 or 70 children being cared for, and most of all being given the love they so badly needed, often having been rejected and banished by relatives earlier on. There were no state funds, and the whole enterprise was a matter of trusting the Lord for daily provision to feed and clothe the children, and to pay their school fees. Many of those children, even those who arrived HIV+, have gone on to become healthy, productive adults, some having been able to go to university or to get other life-skills training. Many have happily come to personal faith and now serve in the churches, having learned to pray, and seeing answers to prayer, in their years at the House of Grace. The story of the House of Grace is reminiscent of the work of George Mueller, whose children's homes in Bristol more than a century before were also founded on trusting God, day by day, for every need. The Ellards remained in Thailand until they were in their 80s, only finally returning to the UK in 2021, to be near some of their own children and grandchildren as they themselves began to need care.

Not everyone went to Asia! Paul Draper went to Mauritius. He had first met and befriended Mauritians before arriving at BTI in 1962, and step by step he became convinced that he should go there. It was to be 1974 before he actually got there, but, in the meantime, he had become Honorary Secretary of the Anglo-Mauritius Society, and worked as Superintendent of the Shaftesbury Mission in Battersea,

London. Finally, he made it to the destination so long prayed for, and along with members of a village church he set up a handicrafts workshop. Four years and many adventures later, and with help from Bishop Trevor Huddleston, he established CRAFT-AID as a rehabilitation and training centre, and production workshop, for people with disabilities.

In 1982, Paul took Mauritian citizenship, and a few years later moved to the Mauritian Island dependency of Rodrigues. Here he was able to set up another workshop and training centre for disabled people. This is independent, but has good relationships with all the established denominations. Paul often visited some of those who had been part of the project after they had left, and tells the story of one amusing incident on such a visit: 'I went to visit old "Bonhomme Ze Ze", who was blind and completely bedridden, yet living on his own in a shack on the summit of a hill outside Port Maturin. I was informed of a death in a hut further down the hillside, and if I had a camera with me, could I go and take a photo of the deceased as his wife had no photo of him. When I arrived at the house, the dead man had been dressed in his wedding suit, shoes and all, and with a flower in his buttonhole. In order to take the photo, he had to be propped up from behind. Unfortunately, at the crucial moment his head slumped over, which rather spoiled the effect. The family was hugely pleased with the result, and the photo was framed.' There are some things that a BTI training couldn't anticipate.

Some students found unusual ways of funding themselves through BTI. David Staveley had learned to fly, with a view to one day being able to join Missionary Aviation Fellowship. He wangled a part-time job, compatible with meticulously completing his BTI studies and outreach responsibilities, flying mail and small packages to the Inner Hebrides and small islands, often having to land on improvised airstrips, fields or beaches. As he said, that was excellent training for service with MAF, whose pilots frequently had to airlift people needing hospital treatment from remote villages or even jungle clearings, or deliver supplies or medicine – or missionaries! – to equally remote places. Andrew MacBeath didn't bat an eyelid at his student's activities, simply mildly enjoined him 'to take care', and said he would pray for his safety.

Dave went to Ethiopia with MAF, and loved it – and met his wife there. They had several more years in Ethiopia, including a stint when Dave was programme manager, and working with people pioneering in remote areas, before the Marxist take-over meant that after a period of increasing restrictions, missionaries were expelled. MAF then asked Dave to develop recruitment and training based in the UK – and to his amusement he often found himself taking pilots-in-training to the same Scottish hills and Hebridean islands that were so familiar to him from his BTI years. Dave was able to continue in this role until his official retirement.

MacBeath would have been glad that he hadn't turned him away as a student who didn't quite fit the usual mould!

Margaret Hill (Wycliffe Bible Translators) training Bible translators in Uganda

Hugh Trevor (OMF) driving gospel van in Japan

Ian Bowley sharing the gospel in Thailand

Margaret Trevor teaching children in Japan

28
Some students who stayed in Britain

ANDREW MacBeath's deep commitment to world mission did not mean that he neglected students who expected to stay in Britain, or in their home countries if they were from overseas. He had a profound belief that what mattered was that each student should be guided by the Holy Spirit, and obedient to that calling, wherever that might be.

From early on in the life of BTI there had been a steady stream of men (always men at that time) who had become pastors of churches at home, or had served in a range of Christian enterprises. In particular, in the early days, that had meant the mission halls (mostly but not exclusively in the cities), the growing number of City Missions, independent fellowships, and a small group of mainstream denominations, notably the Baptists. The Presbyterians and Anglicans/Episcopalians rigidly held to their own training requirements, which involved a university degree and/or (in the case of the Anglicans) a degree course at their own denominational colleges. In their view, BTI did not qualify, often out of ignorance as to how rigorous BTI's courses could be, or because those making the rules were not approving evangelicals. Some men did go on after BTI and take a university degree in order to meet requirements, but until well on into the 1960s, in Britain university was very much for a small number of men, and even fewer women, rarely more than about 5% of young people. Others first pastored where this was not an issue, and then later embarked on the extra training to qualify for formal ordination into a mainline church.

Among those who benefited from more flexible Baptist rules was David Evans, who, with wife Stephanie, who was also a BTI graduate, was called in 1970 to be pastor of Burra Isle Baptist Church in the Shetlands. There they spent five very happy years in a small island community. Subsequently, David pastored Baptist churches in Bathgate and Dundee, before heading back to Bath, where he had grown up, and finally Cullompton in Devon. Succeeding David at Burra Isle was Douglas Crisp, who had been a fellow student at BTI.

After Burra, Douglas pastored Baptist churches in Grangemouth, followed by Tottenham in north east London. For Alex Russell, the route to Baptist ministry was different. He had entered BTI with no formal educational qualifications behind him, but was seen to have much potential. He was nurtured by staff and fellow students so that, by the time he finished his years at BTI he had established sufficiently strong academic foundations to enable him then to go on to the Baptist College, and flourish there. He pastored four Baptist churches in turn in Scotland, followed by one in Kent, before returning to part-time ministry in Edinburgh and Kirkintilloch before full retirement.

Some former students returned to secular jobs, using their BTI training to help them disciple people in their workplaces, and contributing to the local churches where they were members, or interwove church-based ministry with periods back in other work. One couple who did this were Ken and Edith McAuley. After 18 months back in his old trade of joinery, Ken took up a post with Newcastle City Mission. Nine years later they moved to The Vine Street Mission in Gateshead, which became Gateshead Evangelical Church. After six exhausting years they felt they needed a break from full-time church work, and Ken returned once again to joinery, enjoying his time with people who were not part of a church. The McAuleys did not stop witnessing to the Lord, so, after five years, and with a small but growing nucleus of new believers, they decided to plant a new church in a difficult housing scheme where there was no other church. Before long, they were able to establish worship services, work with children, young people, and the elderly, and set up a charity shop.

Quite a few former students went back to teaching or nursing, both of which vocations provided scope both for involvement in a local church but also practical and professional ways of serving others. Sheena Boddington first taught in a primary school in Castlemilk, Glasgow, then spent a year in Oxford studying Chinese. Next came several busy years at L'Abri in Hampshire, a Christian conference and community centre which had its roots in the ministry of Francis Schaeffer. By then the Vietnamese 'boat people' refugees were arriving, and Sheena moved back to primary teaching in order to help their children. Alongside her teaching, Sheena became increasingly involved with international students in Chichester, West Sussex, where she lived at the time, and this in turn led to her moving on to a full-time role, lasting ten years, working with overseas students in Edinburgh as a staff worker for Friends International. She was later to comment, 'I can truly say that God has brought together many disparate strands in my life in a way that has brought much fulfilment amidst its challenges. Nothing has been wasted.'

John Muir had not been a teacher before BTI, but became convinced that primary teaching was to be his future. So, he went on to do the requisite training, met his wife at Hamilton College, and went on to teach in Livingston, where in time he became Assistant Head of his school. Next came an appointment to be Head of a rural primary school near Aviemore, followed by some years as Adviser in Primary Education for the Highland Council. This latter post involved overseeing quality assurance and staff development for Caithness and Sutherland, which brought many opportunities to help teachers keen to do their best for their pupils, and to improve the life chances of many children. Both John and his wife supported Scripture Union groups in schools wherever they could, and in each place where they lived helped with the Sunday School.

For these, and countless others who stayed in Britain, their BTI years helped equip them for fruitful service and effective witness in their professions, neighbourhoods and churches.

29
A new era

I N 1969, Andrew Macbeath retired. He had given unstinting and wise leadership for 15 demanding and change-filled years, and was weary. He also had family responsibilities for which he needed more time. He would be sorely missed, but there was deep thankfulness for all that he had been and all that he had done under God.

Rev. Geoffrey W. Grogan,
BTI Principal 1969-91

It was time to move on once again. The GUEA and BTI Councils quickly, and unanimously, agreed to invite Geoff Grogan to become the new Principal. Grogan was well known and much loved already, he had already spent most of the past 20 years embedded at BTI, and even though at present he was on the staff of London Bible College, where he taught for four years, it seemed likely that he would agree to return and take up this new role. He did. He was to remain in post till 1991.

Grogan was by now an established scholar, especially in his specialist field of Systematic Theology. He was a gifted Bible teacher and preacher, and a caring pastor. He was now well known in England as well as in Scotland, and had friends in networks in Wales and Northern Ireland. Unlike Macbeath, he had no overseas missionary experience, but he had built warm relationships with many an overseas student in past years, and kept up a prodigious correspondence with former students, whether domestic or internationals, wherever they were in the world. His deep concern for the cause of the gospel and the state of the churches in the UK was well matched by his awareness of what was happening globally.

As had been the case for Macbeath, Grogan would go on to oversee numerous changes. Early in his tenure, the basic course was extended from two years to three, though there was flexibility for those who wished to study for shorter periods. This was because there seemed an increasing number of subjects that somehow needed to be accommodated, and also because more students wished to acquire a university-validated qualification alongside the BTI's own syllabus. Visas for service overseas increasingly demanded this, as did schools looking for teachers of Religious Knowledge. It was growing harder to find a post as a pastor without the so-called prestige of a university award. In many spheres of work, beyond the parameters of Christian ministry, the pressure to have a degree or a qualification that was recognised by the State was steadily growing; whether or not that qualification actually increased effectiveness was another question. A real problem for BTI was that university awards related to theology focused on theoretical knowledge, but did not address practical ministry skills and experience.

The London University Certificate and Diploma had been available to BTI students for some years already, and this arrangement lasted till 1977 when the switch was made to the Cambridge Certificate or Diploma in Religious Studies. More and more students opted for this, with the syllabus for various subjects being compatible with BTI's ethos, though this was to become more problematic during the later 1980s. Students taking this also took BTI's own courses which addressed ministry and spiritual development, including ministry placements. For three years, 1978-1981, BTI staff also took extension classes in Dumfries and Kilmarnock, teaching the Cambridge courses, to enable men and women to qualify for teaching Religious Education in schools. For some years, there was also an arrangement with Glasgow Presbytery of the Church of Scotland to run evening classes to train Lay Readers for their churches. A number of African students asked to take the London A-level in Religious Studies, as this was recognised in their home countries, and a handful of British students tagged along. From 1981, the London Bachelor of Divinity course became part of the College's official syllabus, although numbers taking advantage of this were small in relation to the overall student body; those who did, did well, achieving Honours awards. It was not easy, though arguably necessary at the time, to accommodate so many different courses, and the workload for staff was heavy. Further, the pressure was on for Grogan to appoint more specialist lecturers, with matching recognised university qualifications, than had been necessary in the past. This was to cope with the demands of courses designed by universities with dedicated staff in each specific subject within the degree or diploma. It was hard to balance the need for more staff with keeping fees as low as possible. Further, the Library needed constant upgrading and expansion, which was also costly. There was more paperwork and administration, and only so much that lecturers could absorb on top of their increasingly complicated teaching responsibilities. Grogan confessed that he struggled with it all. In addition, he was being asked to serve on various national Boards and committees concerned with education in general or theological and religious education in particular. His workload was very heavy.

At the same time, numbers were falling back to previous levels after the peak figures of the mid-1960s. Through the 1970s, student numbers were mostly between about 90 and 130, though others in addition were still taking evening classes or correspondence courses. Where for much of its earlier years, BTI had been the only real option – certainly the most popular - in Britain for such a training as was offered, the picture by now was far different. All Nations had moved to its home in Easeneye, with its lovely grounds, in 1963; by the 1970s it had assembled a highly gifted team of staff, and was rightly earning a fine reputation for its training in cross-cultural ministry, its main focus. Many students who in the past would probably have gone to BTI now chose All Nations instead. London Bible College by now had world-wide recognition, and many of its staff were known widely in British evangelical circles. There were other Bible Colleges also now established in various parts of the UK.

It didn't help that Glasgow was in trouble as a city. Most of its heavy industries had closed, there was high unemployment, the population was shrinking, and the city was scruffy and rather unattractive compared with what was on offer elsewhere. It didn't help that the original BTI building in Bothwell Street, by now 80 years old, was clearly showing its age. It needed expensive repairs, and upgrading to meet the increasing expectations of a post-war generation whose homes were now often far more comfortable than those of earlier generations.

On a wider front, in British society in general there was an increasing sense of embarrassment, or even outright hostility, in relation to Britain's imperial past. Through the 1960s and 1970s, more and more former colonies gained their independence, even though many chose to remain in the Commonwealth. There were strident voices in some political and academic circles accusing Christian mission of being the tool of imperialism, past and present, and therefore to be condemned. The widespread enthusiasm of a century before, at least in church circles, for missionary activity and support for missionaries, was now often replaced in too many churches by a sense of shame.

As immigration brought people of other faiths increasingly into the lives of many Britons, coupled with radical voices from within the churches themselves and growing boldness of atheist spokespeople, the default belief was that, if you believed in God at all, then 'all religions lead to God'. Mission that involved a call to conversion to Christ, celebrated a century before, was now regarded as outrageous, unethical, or worse. Radio, television and the print media were all moving steadily away from any sense of Christian truth as the basis for contemporary living. The Beatles popularised eastern mysticism in an extraordinarily powerful way, and huge numbers of younger people in particular swallowed this along with their music. The hippie movement, and the sexual revolution, shaped culture very powerfully.

It was a confusing and difficult time for the BTI as the transition to having to be deeply counter-cultural, and even misunderstood or roundly criticised by many churches, shrank its circle of friends. Geoff Grogan and his team were solid in their commitment to biblical truth and to the Person and unique work of Jesus Christ, as only Lord and Saviour. There were many churches that were faithfully true to biblical truth. All the same, it took great grace and courage to keep the BTI ship steady. It was a difficult tightrope to make changes that were necessary and appropriate while also holding fast to what must not be changed. Evangelicals did not always agree where to draw lines, and were sometimes more tribal and less united than before.

30
Despite the challenges, God...

D ESPITE all the challenges, the early decades of Grogan's principalship saw a steady flow of gifted, well-grounded men and women moving on into effective Christian ministry, both in the UK and around the world.

Some were only at BTI for a limited period, but still made their mark. Most memorable of all the short-termers was Chhirc Tiang, perhaps one of the briefest of all students. He was a major in the Cambodian Army, who had been sent to Edinburgh in 1971 for a postgraduate degree in engineering at Heriot Watt University. At the end of his course, with a few weeks to go before his visa expired, he asked if he might spend those last few weeks – just a month in June 1973 – at BTI. He needed, he said, a brief interval to soak himself in Scripture and prayer before returning to Cambodia, which was in turmoil. He was a committed Christian from a large Christian family, and a fearless evangelist and acknowledged Christian leader in a staunchly Buddhist country where at the time the church was still very small. What was God calling him to be and do in these perilous days?

Cambodia was a desperately troubled country politically, and as Chhirc Taing and his wife heard of the growing threat from the murderous Khmer Rouge, Chhirc felt he must return to help his people. He left his wife and baby daughter in Edinburgh, and went back to Phnom Penh, where over the next 18 months he saw thousands coming to faith as he and others witnessed boldly. But in April 1975 the Khmer Rouge over-ran the city and Chhirc was swept up in the brutal results, which ushered in the terrible Pol Pot years. In a short time about two million, out of a total population of about six million, were murdered. Perhaps another two million fled to refugee camps in Thailand and elsewhere. Chhirc was clubbed to death within days of the fall of the capital city, seen still sharing the gospel urgently as he was taken away to his death.

Two BTI students who had been especially gripped by Chhirc's impassioned pleas for prayer and help for Cambodia were Paul and Helen Penfold. Out of those brief weeks of shared life that June came 'Cambodia for Christ', an agency dedicated to raising prayer and aid for that tragic country and its suffering people. This included finding ways to enable surviving Cambodians to be settled in other countries, including the UK. Later, Cambodia for Christ morphed in 1978 into South East Asian Outreach, as sadly Vietnam and Laos also saw huge displacement of population as Communism overtook their countries. Today all three countries have stabilised, with varying degrees of openness to Christian presence, but for each of them there were bitter years of suffering and war. Both believing Cambodians and a number of Christian mission agencies were to play a key role in rebuilding the country after the overthrow of Pol Pot.

There were other students, too, who were never to forget Chhirc and his message. Among them was a group of five couples and one single woman who all completed their courses in 1974 and went with OMF to South East Asia – Thailand, Japan, the Philippines. Two couples, John and Elspeth Taylor and Bob and Jan Trelogan, remained in their respective countries of service till retirement, after which they returned to Glasgow and continued working among international students and immigrants. Ann Stanworth also remained in Asia till retirement. The three other couples returned to Britain after considerable periods in Asia, and all continued in effective ministry in a variety of settings, including ordained ministry in Scotland and working with other mission agencies.

Raised in the Forest of Dean, Charles Price was their contemporary. He was a gifted evangelist and also soon became a much-loved speaker at events such as the Keswick Convention. Together with wife Hilary, Charles was on the staff of Capernwray Bible School for 27 years, including many years as Principal. Word spread about his winsome teaching, and before long he was being asked to speak at conferences and conventions around the world, in time visiting about a hundred countries for Bible ministry. In 2001 Price was called to be Pastor of the very large People's Church in Toronto, Canada, where he remained till retirement in 2016. He was held in such high regard that at his retirement he was sent a video message from the then prime Minister, Justin Trudeau, thanking for his services to the Canadian nation.

Not all BTI graduates had such high-profile ministries as Charles Price! Many became teachers, nurses, doctors or home-makers, using their training to help them continue serving well in local churches and professional spheres. Some such as Chris Jack first became a pastor, then went on to other forms of ministry, in Jack's case becoming Principal of Romsey House, Cambridge, and then Vice-Principal of the London School of Theology.

There were still students coming from abroad. Some Scandinavians, Dutch and German students, and others, such as Milan Tovarloza, from Eastern Europe. Chi Mo Hong came from South Korea and went on to become a Professor of Church History in his home country: Scotland was a favoured destination for training for Koreans because of their shared Presbyterian Church story, and many more Koreans came in the 1980s and 1990s. Pan Chi Khen was from East Malaysia, and went on to a career first in social work and as a local magistrate, and then as pastor of the Glasgow Chinese Church for many years. Clifford Taylor came from Trinidad, and developed as an effective evangelist. He also served as a Baptist minister in London. In1979, the College was enriched by four Nigerians, all sent by SIM (Sudan Interior Mission, later Service in Mission). They were all mature students with considerable ministry experience already, one being the Principal of a Bible College. Istafanus Kpasaba, stayed for a second year. They brought their exuberant worship, far different from the historic sober Presbyterianism so often prevailing in Scotland, and the reality of deep faith in the context of political turmoil and suffering. They also brought experience of the interface, and often confrontation, between Christianity and Islam, as well as an insight into the growing new forms of Christian church springing up across sub-Saharan Africa.

The 1970s saw a growing renewal in British churches, many of which were touched by the Charismatic Movement, and Pentecostal churches were growing too. The Scottish mainstream churches, especially the Presbyterian ones, were in general less impacted by the Charismatic Movement than several English ones, and more cautious about some of its emphases. Influence filtered in via the university Christian Unions, themselves growing rapidly in this period, and by a number of widely popular books and conference speakers, along with a cascade of new Christian songs and hymns and music tapes, and as a result of shared attendance at events such as the Keswick Convention and Spring Harvest. BTI students were affected by all these things, and had to learn to respect and live with those whose views on it all differed from their own. After one difficult period, Grogan had to insist that while lively discussion about things such as speaking in tongues was reasonable, heavy-handed proselytising was forbidden. There needed to be respectful diversity on such matters, just as there was over things such as baptism and church order. It had always been a strength of the College that students came from differing backgrounds and denominations, and that was not to change now.

There was also among British evangelicals a growing recovery of what came to be called the holistic, or integral, gospel, with the recognition that evangelism and social engagement needed to be kept together, and that to do so was not simply embracing liberalism. In the USA, the shadow of the fundamentalist swing of the 1920s and onwards still affected many – even most – evangelicals there, while at the same time the World Council of Churches in this decade became increasingly captive to a highly politicised agenda from which the biblical gospel was sadly too often missing. It was inevitable that suspicion about social engagement deepened in many American churches, and among evangelicals elsewhere. The story in Britain had been rather different, partly because of closer involvement in the reconstruction of Europe following World War II, not to mention the need to rebuild much of Britain itself. Many British evangelicals were equally opposed to the World Council of Churches and its emphases, but much more open to a more holistic faith. The Refugee Council of the Evangelical Alliance in 1968 morphed into what today we know as Tearfund, and in 1969 the Shaftesbury project was established to foster closer political and social engagement, inspired by the 19th century social reformer and deeply committed Christian, Lord Shaftesbury. Even so, the post-war establishing of the Welfare State had perhaps muddied the waters a bit, as traditional expressions of church-based care for the whole person in the whole of life had been taken over by the State – education, medical care, care for the poor and destitute, and innumerable Christian-inspired charities. Not that all churches had done a good job, but the churches as a whole had been at the heart of social engagement, and communities, for centuries. Now this needed to be recovered. At BTI, students were encouraged to explore biblical and theological foundations for integrating evangelism and social action.

On a wider canvas, the Lausanne Congress called in 1974 by Billy Graham was to have huge consequences. Nobody could accuse Graham of being less than totally committed to the need for evangelism, and the Congress did not contradict that, but the revivalist model so often adopted since the nineteenth century needed to be challenged, especially as the Western world moved away from its Christian history and assumptions. How can you revive what has not had life in the first place? Had not too many evangelicals in their commitment to evangelism been guilty of reductionism when ignoring the need for conversion (and active discipleship) in every dimension of life? The Lausanne Covenant which emerged from the Congress, much of it crafted by the gifted London minister of All Souls, John Stott, set out clearly why faithful mission must bring evangelism and social engagement together, not set them in opposition to one another. True conversion, true discipleship, and true church life, needed to be expressed in a holistic and integrated way. Was this not the pattern of the Lord Jesus himself?

Many of the churches of the global south, today usually termed the majority world, and mostly the fruit of western missions, were by now fully adult in their own right. Reflecting the fact that many of their countries were currently breaking away from their colonial past, they were in the best sense more and more confident to raise their voices on the world Christian stage as equals. They also, many of them, came from contexts where poverty, hunger, exploitation, injustice and violence were facts of life. A gospel that only spoke of personal salvation, with nothing much to say about whole-life current realities was not adequate. Nor was it biblical. Their representatives came to Lausanne keen and well able to demonstrate why social engagement was not an add-on but vital to the credibility and faithfulness of the gospel.

Two Latin Americans, Samuel Escobar and Rene Padilla, were especially powerful in the case they made. Both deeply involved in leadership in the student world through IFES (International Fellowship of Evangelical Students), in countries intensely embroiled in the struggle by Marxists to win their peoples from centuries of Roman Catholicism, Escobar and Padilla showed how a pietistic and individualistic form of evangelism simply did not reflect the fullness of the gospel, and provided no answers in the face of such contexts as theirs. Africans and Asians agreed. It was not that there needed to be less evangelism, far from it, but it must be in tandem with social engagement and concern for justice, especially for the poor, and ministering to the whole person in every dimension of life. People needed to see the embodiment of the love and grace and compassion of the Lord, not just hear about it. They needed to see that discipleship involved every area of life, and that the gospel spoke to them all. Transformation is more than a personal ticket to heaven for an individual. Many mission agencies had for generations been deeply involved in a more fully-orbed gospel ministry, bringing medical care and education, attention to sustainable living and family welfare, deliverance from addiction and the fear of malign spirits, along with evangelism and Bible translation, preaching and teaching and the establishing of churches. But more needed to be done, and colleges such as BTI needed to be sure to train students to embrace holistic ministry, even when some more conservative evangelical churches were nervous that such an agenda diluted focus on the atoning death of Christ and the centrality of new birth. But, making disciples was about more than an individual's reconciliation with God through personal faith in Christ, whilst certainly not less. BTI also drew attention to more and more non-western voices as journals and books written by global south Christians became increasingly available, and steadily more available in English. Lecturers had to be on their toes to incorporate some of this rich resource into their teaching.

It was more and more evident that God was building His Church on every continent and that what – sometimes patronisingly – had often been referred to as 'the young churches', were increasingly mature, able in their own right to engage in deep theological and biblical reflection, and rightly expected to be treated as equals and with respect. Where a century before, westerners were mostly the pioneers and leaders, and 'in charge', now they needed more and more to embrace with humility the leadership and direction of national believers in the different countries of the majority world. While there were still plenty of places and people groups who needed pioneers, increasingly what was needed were missionaries who could work humbly alongside or under national believers. The shape of cross-cultural mission was changing. Any sense of colonial mentality must go.

Rubbing shoulders with students from the global south – Africa, Asia, Latin America – meant that BTI's community could not ignore these winds of change. There must be expectation to learn from believers in different parts of the world as well as from those of different denominations within the 'old countries'. That applied to life within the BTI community as well as in preparing men and women for service beyond.

31

Another transition

BY the late 1970s it was clear that the Bothwell Street BTI building was no longer viable. It needed major and expensive repairs and upgrading, and more students wanted to live in student flats or, if married, needed different kinds of accommodation and lifestyle than could be afforded by the old building. While the GUEA Board (who were still the umbrella above the BTI Council), were pondering what to do and when, the Glasgow City Council announced plans to build an inner ring road, supplementing the highly valuable M8 motorway, which ran through the city but mostly at a distance from the centre, and the proposed route would involve demolition of some existing buildings. This included the BTI and its adjoining premises.

The inner ring road was never built, and the BTI building and those adjoining it were taken over by a developer, but while the plan was still in place it became clear that BTI must move, and as soon as possible. As was common practice, the anticipated compulsory purchase order meant that little money could be raised on selling the old building, and there were almost no reserves, for the GUEA or for BTI. The challenge seemed insurmountable. The GUEA itself was contracting: many of its former social amelioration and medical ministries had been replaced by State provision or were no longer viable, many of the mission halls had either morphed into independent evangelical churches or closed as areas of old tenements were pulled down, and there were no longer wealthy sponsors to supply funds. The GUEA had served a worthy purpose for close on a century, but was now left with a much-diminished role.

It was clearly a time for urgent and persistent seeking for guidance. After much prayer and much searching, George Bryson, Secretary of the GUEA at the time, and BTI leaders, were led to the Kelvinside Church, which, with a dwindling congregation, was being merged with another church, Hillhead Church of Scotland, nearby and so was available for sale. It stood at the junction of Great Western Road and Byres Road, opposite the main entrance to the Botanic Gardens, in the West End of the city. It had been built and opened as Kelvingrove Botanic Church in 1862, commissioned and paid for by John Blackie, an influential Christian publisher committed to publishing books faithful to Scripture, and who lived nearby in Kew Terrace. As Glasgow expanded westwards, he was eager to provide for a gospel witness in the area. For a long time, it was to be a beacon for truth, with only four ministers in its 116 years as a church.

At the time of Moody's memorable and influential campaign, it had been used as the place where believers from many churches gathered together, night after night. They gave themselves to pray for men and women to come to saving faith as Moody preached, especially on that last extraordinary night when the crowds were so large the meeting had been moved from Glasgow Green to the more spacious Botanic Gardens. It was recorded that many prayed that night that the impact of the campaign would bless the whole world as newly converted men and women went on to take the gospel far and wide. Long after the Moody campaigns were over, the church had maintained its prayer that they should serve the cause of the Kingdom of God worldwide as well as locally.

If BTI had to move, it was good to move to a place where earnest prayer had been made for exactly the outcomes the College had, under God, been called to fulfil, and that were still its vision. It was a shared legacy. God was graciously answering the prayers both of that congregation, past and present, and of the BTI community.

So, during the summer vacation of 1980 a number of former and current students with appropriate skills in the building trades joined forces with a sympathetic firm of contractors to transform the church into the shape it would need to be for its new use. Since the church had lofty ceilings a strongly reinforced upper floor was added at church balcony level which was amongst other things to house the growing library – a heavy load for any floor! Extensive re-wiring had to be done, and sufficient toilets added. Staff studies were constructed in the two side aisles of the lower part of the church, with the large space between as the assembly hall for meetings of the whole College body, daily worship, and lunchtime seating, as well as special events for the public. A kitchen was added, various spaces turned into three classrooms, and areas converted into offices: one for the Principal and one for the administrative office, the latter for years to be the domain of the much loved and seemingly indefatigable former student Vera Waddleton. There was an office for the GUEA Secretary, George Bryson. Upstairs, tucked into the eaves, was a small flat, initially for the Grogans and their family, and then for the Waddleton family, who were able to serve as caretakers along with their multitude of other roles. It was amazing what you could fit into one large and lofty nineteenth century church building!

The teams rushing to complete painting and last-minute joinery were working right to the last day before the new term began, but as the doors opened to the intake of students for the new academic year everything was in place to welcome them, with only a handful of outstanding minor tasks. It had been an impressive team effort, and there was much praise to the Lord that all had been accomplished, on time, and without accidents. It had also been done with comparatively little expense, thanks to so much voluntary labour.

There was no residential accommodation, as by now few wanted it, though a couple of small self-catering residences were set up for those without local options. Many students lodged with their own or local families, or arranged their own rented accommodation. There are both gains and challenges about living in a close residential community, and perhaps over the years more students were to adopt a commuter mentality rather than the deep inter-dependence of the former model. It also made it harder to include in-house evening activities, and some students rightly or wrongly reckoned only to be in college for lectures. But, for more and more students it met the reality of changing culture. It also enabled more students to be more firmly embedded in a local church community, and for married staff and students to have more family life. It made it possible for more part-time students to join in, and for others to take part-time employment to pay their fees and living costs.

Some staff carried on from their service at the former site, others were appointed in the years ahead. Among those who continued were Richard Thomas who had joined the staff in 1978. He was half-Armenian, and had lived and worked in Lebanon for some years before arriving at BTI. Grogan had met him long before as a fellow-student at London Bible College, and much later invited him to come to teach particularly on non-Christian religions and some missionary subjects. He also taught Arabic to students heading for the Middle east and North Africa as well as teaching Arabic at Glasgow University. He retired in 1991. Frank and Vera Waddleton had both been former students, and joined the staff in 1971, Vera in the office and sharing catering as well; Frank, a former engineer, was warden at Bothwell Street and also responsible for the Correspondence Courses. He went on to lecture in Christian Ethics as well as later helping the college through the complex process of developing, and getting accreditation for, its own degree. David Edwards had also started at Bothwell Street, teaching Old Testament and Church History; he continued right up till his death in 1982. Roy Kearsley, a recent addition to the staff at Bothwell Street, was a former WEC missionary in Ghana, and lectured in Systematic Theology; he brought great skill later as Course Leader at the time (1989-92) the College was designing its own BA degree to meet changing needs. Kearsley left in 1999 to teach at Cardiff University and South Wales Baptist College. Both these men gained PhDs while teaching at BTI, as did David Graham, a Church of Scotland minister, who arrived in 1982 to teach Old Testament, switching to New Testament in 1989. He returned to parish ministry in 1998. Other staff, too, were added in coming years, and many of them also were to win post-graduate awards during their time as lecturers. Among them were Ted Herbert, a former banker, who became a specialist in the Dead Sea Scrolls, and arrived to teach Old Testament. He went on to become Vice-Principal of International Christian College, the final evolution of BTI, and was much mourned when he died in harness of cancer. Another was Rory Mackenzie, who had been a student at BTI in the 1970s, and after years as a missionary in Thailand, was appointed to teach pastoral studies and to oversee all practical placements. But this was further down the line……..

32

Let the children come to Me

FROM BTI's early years, many students had gone on to work with children, whether through Sunday Schools, or evangelistic camps, or working with the poor or handicapped. In time, many more would teach in primary or secondary schools, or work with organisations such as Scripture Union or other organisations devoted especially to reaching and discipling children. Until the 1960s there were still many children in British churches; after that, those numbers slowly dwindled. Today sadly there are many churches in the UK that have no children present at Sunday services, although initiatives such as Messy Church reach some young families, often meeting on a weekday. Sadly, in Scotland many sports activities for children, run by secular clubs, now choose Sunday morning for their events and matches, which presents a dilemma for families who might otherwise be in church.

After World War II especially, a number of organisations specifically addressing discipling or caring for children either began or grew considerably. Part of this was in recognition of the struggles to ensure really good Sunday School teaching in local churches, and also adapting to the takeover of many schools from the churches that had founded them by the State system. In theory a level of religious education of a strongly Christian character, together with Christian assemblies, was supposed to be guarded, especially in primary schools, but in practice this was increasingly challenged as more teachers and the education unions adopted a non- or even anti- Christian stance. Further, the UK was becoming increasingly multi-cultural, with immigrants arriving from many faith backgrounds, and they often objected to specifically Christian dominance of content. For the many BTI graduates who went on to teach in schools in the UK, whether religious education or some other subject, they were more and more on the front line of a mission field, and as in most mission fields, with considerable obstacles to surmount. Scripture Union and other organisations worked hard to reach children, in school and out, and many a BTI graduate offered help with lunchtime meetings where they were permitted, and with summer camps.

Among those who went on to work with children in other ways were a number who became involved with, or set up, orphanages in needy parts of the world, especially in Africa. Katie MacKinnon, who had been a student at BTI in the mid-1960s, went in 1972 to Kenya with the Africa Inland Mission. She was a nurse, with a huge heart for babies and young children. After a while, posted to a rather remote Kipsigis tribal area, she discovered that in the local culture premature babies or babies born to uncircumcised young girls were regarded as non-persons, and must be left to die or even actively smothered. Even the local staff in the clinic shared that belief, or at least could not stand against it, even when they claimed to be Christians. Katie was horrified, and greatly distressed. To her, these were still precious babies, who deserved the very best care until they were strong enough to thrive as much as any other child.

At first, unable to persuade the local staff to change their ways, Katie simply took more and more of these small babies into her own small home, and cared for them devotedly, often having to be up most of the night as well as through the day to feed and change these tiny people. Miraculously, friends in Glasgow arranged for an incubator to be delivered to her remote location, which arrived at a particularly critical moment, and now she was able to give the best medical care to the most premature babies. A little later, a Dutch foundation offered to underwrite the cost of setting up a dedicated children's home, the costs of supporting each child there, and the expense of appointing full-time staff. Step by step, God lovingly ensured that what had seemed so impossible should become thoroughly established, and in due course countless babies and small children would be rescued. Soon the Dutch were supporting a chain of centres for the care of babies and children, and a few years later a large, purpose-built Baby Home was added to the tally. To this day, this ministry continues. One woman's passionate love for the utterly defenceless has been used by the Lord to transform the lives of thousands.

Nearly 30 years after Katie had been at BTI, Allan and Jacqui McKinnon also became students at what by now had become Glasgow Bible College. They, too, shared a deep love for children, and went to Moshi, Tanzania, to serve with the Moshi Christian Children's Centre. As in Kenya, there are multiple reasons why so many small children need care: mothers dying giving birth, parents dying of AIDs, famine, traditional superstitions about premature babies or twins, and a host more.

A Quantity Surveyor by background, Allan had first worked in Tanzania for three years, seconded from Scripture Union Scotland to oversee the building of a permanent camp-site and conference centre for SU Tanzania. This had given him and Jacqui, a nurse, a great love for the people there, and ample opportunity also to observe needs in the country. That love has never left them, even when back in Scotland for a season for their own children's education. It took them back to found and lead the Berea Bible School, also in Moshi, while continuing to be deeply involved in the Children's Centre. Back in Scotland once more, they first joined the staff of the Brethren GLO Centre in Motherwell and the Tilsley College which is part of that, and in due course Allan became Principal. During all these moves, Jacqui exercised her gifts in caring medically and pastorally for staff and students, and ministry through initiatives such as Christians Against Poverty, while Allan, a persistent student, combined training others with several post-graduate courses including a PhD. He would say that his passion has been to train men and women, in Scotland and Africa, to keep deepening their understanding of Scripture, and the skills to teach it faithfully and accurately, while growing steadily in spiritual character: a close mirror of the goals that lay behind the creation of the BTI, and its vision ever since.

Another couple whose love for children shaped their lives were Katsumi and Keiko Takagi. In Japanese culture, there is strong religious resistance, related to the importance of ancestral lines and practices, to the adoption of abandoned or unwanted children, especially of babies born to unmarried mothers or those of mixed race. As a matter of Christian conviction, the Takagis, unable to have a child of their own, had themselves adopted a baby boy, who as a toddler accompanied them to Glasgow and quickly won the hearts of fellow students and church family alike. During and after World War 2, there were many babies born in numerous countries who had been fathered by servicemen of occupying armies, and sadly foreign workers have continued that pattern for many years. Japan was no exception. There were also genuine orphans, whose parents had both died, and whose relatives were unable to take them in. The international

The Takagi family: Katsumi became Asia Director of World Vision

ministry, World Vision, had been established in response, and the Takagis had been deeply moved by their work in Japan, hence their adoption of Motoi.

They had both learned some English before arriving in Scotland, especially Katsumi, but even so it was hard to keep abreast of lectures and essays, and very tiring. But, they persevered, and fellow-students often stepped in to help, as had been the college pattern for years with overseas students for whom working in English was difficult. Courses completed, and facility in English much improved, they returned to Japan where Katsumi joined the staff of World Vision. In time he became a senior member of staff for the whole of East Asia. His focus remained on caring for children, whatever the reason for their having no family of their own. The church in Japan is very small, but the impact of World Vision and the service of the Takagis has encouraged other Japanese Christians to dare to adopt a needy child, even those with handicaps, and to show the transformative love of Christ in so doing. Now retired, they are quietly planting a church in a remote area.

Kathryn and Ken Cloke, as many another couple, met at BTI. After a stint in India, they returned eight years later to what was by then Glasgow Bible College to upgrade their Cambridge Diplomas to the recently accredited Honours Degree. Their further years of study were to set the direction of their future ministry. Kathryn wrote in a reflective paper: 'Another question which especially concerns me is that of the place of the poor and marginalised of the world in God's purposes. This is another area which I feel was previously hidden from me, partly from my own perspective of being one of the rich of the world, and also partly because of the church's lack of teaching about the biblical emphasis on the poor and needy......I now believe that God will use me in whatever ministry he sees fit, not based on my gender, but based on the gifts and abilities which he gives me, and on the needs around me.'

When it became possible, and with their vision shared with church and friends, the Clokes moved in 2000 to Romania, together with their three children. Romania had suffered badly under Soviet control,

Kathy Cloke with street people in Romania

and there were countless thousands of street children, and many marginalised groups such as the Romany people. There was no question about the pressing need for work among them. So many children were homeless, hungry and dirty, and with all the temptations of the genuinely penniless – and unloved. Too often the only option was taking to crime or being caught up in sex trafficking. The Clokes set up a charity, 'Vis de Copil' (A Child's Dream), and passionately shared their vision with friends back home and such local people as showed any interest. As the work developed God answered prayer to buy and renovate a building as an established centre. Here children could come for hot food, showers and fresh clothes, somewhere to wash clothes, to be loved and listened to, have a basic education, and to be safe. All priceless gifts if your only experience has been feral life on the streets.

Step by step the centre was able to expand what it could offer, and volunteers came and helped, too, along with a small permanent staff. Such damaged children bring endless problems with them, but gradually some were able to gain the stability and skills they needed to go on to honest employment and dignified life. It was always clear that this was done in the name of the Lord Jesus, but those of all faiths and none were welcomed equally. Love was unconditional. The centre gave (and gives) a voice to street people too often regarded more as vermin than as people. Even though the Clokes had to return to Scotland for health reasons (Kathryn sadly died of cancer in 2021), their legacy is a living, dynamic testimony to God's love for children, and for the very poor. They were able to pass the leadership of the centre on into the hands of those who are equally committed to the vision. The centre continues.

33

More stories from the 1970s and '80s

MANY a former student would testify that they had to work very hard at BTI/ GBC. It was demanding to keep up with lectures, reading and essays, especially for those whose educational background was more limited. During the 1980s, as the coal pits and other heavy industries closed down, there were a number of men who had

Joyce Swan, with Friends International and Heriot Watt University chaplaincy, Edinburgh

'gone down the pits' or to work in the shipyards as teenagers with only the sketchiest of schooling behind them, who came to BTI as mature students because they believed the Lord was calling them to a new life of ministry. Geoff Grogan believed passionately that such people should be welcomed and nurtured, in the tradition of the original founding of the college all those years before. There were special additional classes for those who needed it, teaching basics of good grammar, spelling and organising material for essays. These men might have the broadest of accents, and retain all the chirpiness of the Scottish equivalent of London sparrows, but Grogan rightly saw that they could communicate powerfully with a sector of the population which was largely missing from the churches. It was rewarding to see how many of them blossomed, and went on to fruitful ministry in City Missions or as pastors of the remaining mission halls or to work among alcoholics and drug addicts.

It was deeply satisfying to see them achieve certificates or diplomas, something they might never have previously dreamed to be possible. There were others for whom academic study came more easily, but for whom there was a long path to reach their goal. One such was Eddie Adams, who initially enrolled in evening classes in 1984, while working in his father's civil engineering business. The following year he became a full-time student, and spent four years gaining first the Cambridge Diploma and then the London BD degree. Not content with that, he went straight on to Glasgow University to do a PhD, during which time he also did some teaching at BTI/GBC. By 1996, he was lecturing part-time at King's College, London, while also doing some teaching at London Bible College. Three years later he was full-time at King's, where he in time became a Senior Lecturer, also serving on the Tyndale House Council, Cambridge. It's amazing where humble evening classes might lead! There were others who moved into theological education, after some other ministry. Such a couple was Les and Wapke Henson. He, too, had previously worked in the coal industry before attending BTI. After graduation in 1976 they joined World Team and spent the next 19 years in church planting among the Momina people of West Papua, Indonesia. There they saw a people movement, in which the Lord brought very large numbers of tribal people to faith in Christ. Then, sent by World Team to Australia, Les visited many Bible and Theological colleges throughout Australia, until appointed in 1998 to a full-time post at Tabor College, Melbourne, Victoria. Through his experience of working, with nationals, on a contextual theology for the Melanesian people, he went on to lead Tabor's School of Theology, strongly shaped by his missiology.

Jan Trelogan with students in central Thailand

Bob Trelogan Bible teaching in Central Thailand

After three years at BTI, David Sutherland went directly to France in 1980, following in the steps of a number of former BTI graduates who had also served there. After many years of ministry there, alongside his French wife, Brigitte, whom he met and married there in 1984, Sutherland was to reflect, 'France's reputation as being "the missionaries' cemetery" is not too

Rory Mackenzie teaching in Thailand

much of an exaggeration'. Despite the uphill nature of gospel ministry in France's context, the Sutherlands were to see growth in each of the areas where they served, with congregations established and believers strengthened. In each place, God gave them a 'key couple' – men and women born and brought up in that town or region, and with large networks of family and friends. These became the key to the growth of the church. The Sutherlands also had responsibility for the Emmaus Bible correspondence courses for France and Belgium, with some French-speaking students enrolling from other parts of the French-speaking world. This course caters for hundreds of students year by year, and contributes significantly to the faith journey of many people.

For Alison (Hendrie) Mackay, it was a much longer journey to reach her destination. Having been convinced the Lord was calling her to work with Russians almost from her conversion as a teenager, she arrived at BTI in 1976 while still only 18. At the time, Russia was tight shut to foreigners, and most certainly to foreign missionaries, so how would she get there? BTI course completed, and after topping up her Highers, Alison went to Glasgow University to study Russian language: another five years, including one in Russia courtesy of the British Council. Another year for teacher training……. Then a year teaching English in a state school in Moscow, just as perestroika was beginning. Back home, she met Norrie, a graduate of Northumbria Bible College. They married, joined WEC (World Evangelisation Crusade), and as the USSR unravelled, went to Central Asia to a Russian-speaking country. Later they went to the Baltic region, and engaged in mission mobilisation of Russian-speaking believers. Sometimes in our impatient world it helps to remember that Moses was 80 years 'in the making' before he became the leader of God's people!

There were many from this time who became pastors, full-time evangelists, church pioneers, and crucial lay leaders. Among them was Fred Drummond, who, after BTI went on to ordination, and later, after local church ministry, became the head of Evangelical Alliance, Scotland. His BTI years gave him exposure to working alongside men and women from many different denominations and backgrounds, focusing on so much that unites us rather than on denominational distinctions. Geoff Grogan, a Baptist, was a wonderful model in this, and many students learned from him to respect those with whom they might disagree over secondary issues. Those cross-denominational friendships were to stand Fred in good stead in his later work with EA, with personal links with many churches with BTI connections.

34

The next chapter

I N 1990, Geoff Grogan retired. He had been at the heart of BTI life since his own student days way back in the 1940s, and apart from six years at London Bible College, two as a student and four as a lecturer, he had poured out his life into the well-being of the college. For much of that time, his wife, Eva, also a former BTI student, had also been very active in serving the college, at times on staff and then as a total support to her husband. Together they also kept up an enormous correspondence with former students, which was to continue till Geoff's death in 2011. Few who listened to him as Bible teacher and theology lecturer, or experienced his wise pastoral counsel, or read one of his considerable output of books, could ever forget this godly man.

Peter White,
BTI Principal 1990-96

Now the baton of the role of Principal was passed on to Peter White. Originally training as a vet at Glasgow University's Vet School, White had subsequently responded to God's call and trained as a Church of Scotland minister. He and wife Liz spent 16 years in Edinburgh, leading a housing scheme parish, among people who were often socially and economically disadvantaged in a widely prosperous city. This was immersive practical ministry! At the same time, Peter had retained a strong interest in ongoing study and was gifted academically, keeping abreast of current scholarship. He arrived at a critical turning point for BTI.

For some years there had been frequent discussion about the possibility of BTI developing its own accredited degree. Both Cambridge and London courses had served well in their time, but as the universities moved away from many of the traditional biblical roots of theological training, there were some emphases on these courses which left some staff and students, and the destinations to which they went, a bit uneasy. Further, they did not train people in practical ministry, and their courses were increasingly geared to the interests of students of all faiths or none.

It seemed now was the moment to take the plunge, and devise a degree that fully integrated the academic and the practical (as, for instance, social work or medical training had to do), with emphasis, too, on spiritual formation. At the same time, there was considerable disquiet over the continuing structure of the GUEA, which left the BTI Board underneath the GUEA Board. Sometimes, it seemed, the worthy (and mostly elderly!) gentlemen on that Board had rather lost touch with the realities of theological education in a fast-changing world and equally often changing church scene, both in Britain and around the globe. It caused a measure of tension in both directions, and had it not been for Grogan's grace and peace-making, it would surely have ended in outright explosion. The GUEA was itself finding it very hard to adjust to changes in the requirements for the ministries it had for so long been engaged in. There was no question as to the contribution that had been made in the past, both evangelistically and in a variety of social amelioration ministries, but the Welfare State now (at least in theory!) supplied what was needed in the latter, and was increasingly suspicious of independent work that did not come under their umbrella. Legislation was steadily more onerous, and hard for small charities to comply with. Fewer churches or individuals were willing to support something that, they reasoned, was already being financed through taxes. Some of the old ways of evangelism, for instance street preaching, campaigns, or door-to-door visiting of those beyond the churches, was increasingly unpopular, certainly among those at the receiving end, but also among church people. The Charity Commission's requirements also became increasingly detailed and the GUEA was caught up in them, even though by now most of its ameliorative work was quite limited.

So, with some reluctance, but with dawning realism, the GUEA Board in late 1990 handed over such very limited funds and resources as they still had to BTI, which now became the Glasgow Bible College Association, with the college responsible for establishing new lectureships in Evangelism and in Social Care. This was with a view to training men and women specifically in these areas and thus equipping a new generation to work in new ways. It also ensured these areas were embedded in the training for all students.

Peter White began his tenure as this historic change was being agreed. At the same time, the academic staff had been working hard at designing a new degree course, which was granted validation in January 1992. Initially this was under the auspices of The Council for National Academic Awards (CNAA), but on the demise of that body soon after, the validation passed to the Open University. The new degree was modular in structure, with core modules every student took, and then a considerable range of options. This enabled students to have a firm grounding in basic areas essential to any type of ministry, while also giving the possibility of specialising according to expected future ministry. Practical ministry and attention to spiritual formation were part of the core, as were Bible, theological and some history and pastoral studies. The timetable was also constructed in such a way, with every module scheduled for a complete morning or afternoon weekly for a term, that part-time students could more easily combine study with employment or family responsibilities, or could take a particular course they were interested in. It was very flexible, but hard work – for students and staff alike. It also required meticulous record-keeping as there were so many variations.

The new courses came on stream in the autumn of 1992. In addition to continuing students and completely new students, there were a considerable number of former students who returned to upgrade their Cambridge Diplomas to a BA or BA Honours. There were also missionaries on leave, or UK-based Christian workers, who could come for a term, for instance, for a refresher course. In line with Scottish university tradition, and in distinction from English practice, the complete course right through to an Honours degree took four years, but students could exit after one year with a Certificate, or two years for a Diploma, with three years for a BA, and four years for a BA Honours. Some students with prior qualifications, for instance a degree in another subject, or who already had the Cambridge Diploma, could move into a higher year rather than starting at year one. This ensured maximum flexibility for students, and many took full advantage of it.

As before, every student was assigned to a personal tutor, whose task now was not only pastoral oversight but also to keep a careful watch on each one as he or she threaded the way through the many possible permutations, and to advise on what would best meet the needs of each one's intended future ministry. Most tutors now met each one in their assigned group about once a week, whether briefly or for some more extended discussion, and for prayer. The principal, in the same way as his predecessors, also spent many hours in personal counselling and advising. While university cohorts on courses were often now numbered in hundreds or even more, making individual care for students increasingly impossible, the close personal support at GBC was a significant strength, though some students probably didn't fully appreciate the privilege at the time. For some, this element, together with weekly outside speakers – the descendant of the former specifically missionary meetings – plus some times of common worship and prayer, in addition to the academic work, seemed rather a burden, and each year there was a small minority who complained about it. On the other hand, many a former student retained real affection for the staff who had invested so much in them, and appreciated the stress on the full roundedness of training.

All this innovation meant the library needed to expand greatly, which it was able to do under the watchful competence of a professional librarian, Janet Watson. In fact, so good did the library become that increasingly students from the university, church ministers and other Christian workers, would buy a modestly priced annual ticket and then make full use of all that was on offer. There was a steadily growing range of books by evangelical scholars, reflecting the growth in evangelical scholarship, and also a developing collection of works in English by scholars and Christian leaders from the global south: Africans, Asians, Latin Americans. The library was not limited to materials written by evangelicals, but also carried a wide range of books from the wider Christian spectrum. It was important for students to interact with material that challenged their own convictions, helping them to understand the wider church better without losing their own faith. Certain books had to be ring-fenced as 'not to be borrowed', especially if they were core texts for current modules, but could be read on-site. Before long, and involving a huge amount of work, with the beginnings of computer use, it was possible to borrow and return books using the electronic system, which freed the librarian from the age-old practice of manually stamping each one on its way in or out.

The staff, too, had the first generation of Amstrad computers in their studies. They were quite limited in what they could do, but were useful all the same. Very, very few students yet had access to their own computers, and laptops were still mostly a distant dream (there were a few around, but at unreachable expense); so, lecture notes had to be taken down by hand and essays appeared in varying degrees of legibility for staff to mark, unless something was written on a typewriter.

Within a surprisingly short time, computers became less eye-wateringly expensive, and able to do more, so that by the end of the 1990s quite a few students had access to one. Today, much material is available on-line, and in Britain at least university students are required to have their own computers; but physical books and libraries are still hugely important. By the turn of the new century, having one's own computer or laptop had become essential rather than a desirable luxury, and staff had to move on from those early versions to much more sophisticated machines. Upgrading computer systems throughout the college became a repeated and considerable expense, bringing more financial pressure on already stressed funds.

David and Lorna Ferguson (OMF), church
planting in Japan

John Richards (OMF) ministering to Mangyan minority people groups, Mindoro, Philippines

Paula Richards (OMF) crossing a river in flood with Filipino Mangyan minority people

35
Serving in hard places

THROUGHOUT the history of BTI, and then GBC, and latterly in the ICC years, the wider world experienced political and religious upheavals. After World War 2, there was a resurgent national and religious confidence among many Islamic countries, often benefiting economically from the boom in oil revenues, but also in India with its huge Hindu majority. In many countries, too, the coming of independence was often achieved with considerable bloodshed, and since it was primarily the European (at least theoretically Christian) powers that had been expanding their empires since the early nineteenth century (with trade links, often exploitative, going further back still), it was easy for resistance to them politically to include resistance to the Christian churches and their faith. This was despite the fact that many missionaries advocated strongly for independence, and for justice for national populations, including openly criticising the way so much trade and local leadership was weighted in favour of the occupying power. The Communist world, too, notably China and the USSR, often brutally repressed the churches. Totalitarian atheism does not look favourably on Christianity. Many believers migrated to where there was greater freedom, but others remained, and, despite suffering, in most places the church was not stamped out. However, fewer BTI graduates, along with other Christian workers, were able to obtain visas for service in many countries to which in the past many had gone.

Where in earlier generations, BTI graduates had been among those who went freely to serve in these countries, or indeed had come from them, it became increasingly hard to enter them for any overtly Christian or church-related purpose. There were sometimes openings to teach in a university or college, or to work in business, or in some still-needed profession such as medical specialities, or to teach English. This involved extra years in secular training and proven professional experience, so that more of those called by God to such places wished to limit the time at Bible College to the shortest possible course. In any case, there were situations where having to account for time at a theological or Bible College on a CV made it harder to obtain a visa. BTI/GBC ran correspondence courses, which could be studied concurrently with secular employment, but they were mostly at a more introductory level; it was not feasible to introduce a whole range of materials at a higher academic level for a limited number of people, especially as some other colleges had already made such provision, and it would not be helpful to compete.

Despite all this, a small stream of students went on to serve in the Islamic world and other hard places. In the past, students had gone to, and come from, such countries, including a number who themselves had been converted from another world religion, or who came from a small Christian minority in a place with an overwhelming majority of another faith, such as Pakistan or Lebanon. Now, in the 1970s to 1990s at least five or more couples and several singles went, for instance, to Mediterranean and North African countries, quietly supporting local believers, running Bible correspondence courses (to which many applied), helping develop literature, doing Bible translation, running health clinics, running businesses, and much more. This was often alongside a secular professional job, and doing that well. Others went to Muslim Asia – Indonesia, central Asia, western China. Others again worked among Muslims in Britain and Europe. Some found openings in contested areas of sub-Saharan Africa where Islam and Christianity are often

Mary Gardner, Bible translator and trainer, killed in bomb explosion in Jerusalem

locked in conflict. These were hard places indeed. Sometime conflict followed a person unexpectedly. Mary Gardner was killed in Jerusalem in March 2011 when Palestinian terrorists blew up the bus in which she happened to be travelling. Mary, from Orkney, had been at BTI 1985-88, and then in 1989 gone to Togo with Wycliffe Bible Translators, where she worked as a Bible translator and consultant. She especially worked on the Ife Bible, but also taught New Testament Greek to African colleagues, and conducted literacy classes so that local Christians in particular should be able to read God's Word for themselves. Having completed the New Testament, living for considerable periods in the remote area of Togo where the Ife people lived, she had gone to Jerusalem to do some further intensive Hebrew studies, to help with Old Testament translation. Her death was a stark reminder that Christians are called to suffer as well as to rejoice.

Since the earliest days of BTI, students had come from Russia and a number of Eastern European countries. In the wake of the Russian Revolution in 1917, and then with the post-World War II development of the USSR and the implementation of the Iron Curtain, this two-way movement largely stopped. Just slipping in ahead of the clampdown was Noemi Stifterova from Czechoslovakia. Before the war, a Scottish missionary from Glasgow, James A Stewart, travelled widely in Eastern Europe, and for a period worked with Noemi's grandfather in Prague. Many people were being converted, and it was a precious partnership.

As soon as possible after the War, Stewart returned to Prague to see how the church had fared. It had been bombed, and Noemi had been badly injured. Stewart took her back with him to Glasgow in order for her to have some plastic surgery, and to learn English. Before returning home, Noemi spent the academic year 1947-48 at BTI. Back home, she married her pastor fiancé, and had two children. She became in her own right a well-known Bible teacher. Her children said that all their childhood Noemi would regale them with stories from her time at BTI, including accidentally setting off a fire extinguisher and covering herself in foam, just before she was due to have an interview with Andrew MacBeath. Instead of rebuking her, MacBeath offered her some tranquillising medicine! She cherished her Certificate, and protected it when soldiers came searching her home. Even more, she cherished all that she had learnt.

Noemi's son, Milan Nemec, became the leader of the Church of the Brethren in Kolin, with care for several congregations, which were often the target of Russian aggression. He was to say: 'The time of communist oppression was especially not an easy period of testing our faith and hope. But, looking back, we remember again how great was God's grace'. Through all those years, Milan and his mother held on to the hope that one day Milan would be able to go to BTI for himself, to see what had so deeply impacted her life. After the Iron Curtain lifted in 1989 and the country became the Czech Republic, Milan seized the first opportunity to come to Glasgow, and spent a joyous year at the college. As a man distilled by suffering, and with years of accumulated pastoral wisdom, he was a great blessing to staff and students alike. His love for the Lord shone through him.

He returned to Kolin for more fruitful years as a pastor, and in 1996 he wrote that so many were joining the church that 'during worship-services we don't have enough space and children have to sit under the pulpit. Praise God, the sowing brings fruit'. Together with two friends, Milan also went to Ukraine where 'we were able to help people living in worse conditions than people in our land. We were able to give a lot of financial and material help to unbelievably poor families, especially widows with many children, and to a small hospital, where people die because there are no antibiotics. If the Lord wills, I hope we can do even more next year.' Sadly, a year or two later Milan died suddenly of a heart attack. Meanwhile, Noemi, despite already being elderly, and Milan's sister, raised funds to buy a large property which had been occupied by Russian army officers and their families, and converted it into a home for 80 old people, homes for four families where a parent or child had a handicap, and another for foster families. Milan's sister wrote that this fulfilled a long-standing dream of her mother, Noemi, and flowed directly from the latter's faith, shaped at least in part by that year at BTI.

36
Another transition

AFTER the early rush of students taking advantage of the new degree programme, including a considerable number who were upgrading from previously awarded Diplomas, as the 1990s moved on numbers fell again gradually. Other interdenominational evangelical colleges were also experiencing falling numbers, and some were in considerable financial difficulty. Later, the specifically denominational colleges were to have the same experience, though mostly financially cushioned by support from their respective denominations. College principals from the similar colleges from across the UK had for years been meeting annually, as had a number of college bursars, and now one option being seriously considered was the possible merger of some of them.

In Scotland, on the whole the churches had never been very good at supporting the college's central needs financially, and some

Tony Sargent,
ICC Principal 1998-2009

did not even significantly support their own church members who came to study. As many Scottish churches found themselves with falling numbers, there was even less appetite for helping GBC, even when there was recognition of the value of the training, from which so many congregations had benefited hugely.

In 1996 Peter White returned to parish ministry, and while discussions about the future of the college were becoming more pressing, recently retired academic Alex McIntosh was appointed as acting principal, a role he held for two eventful years. He led a gifted and highly committed staff team, and won the respect of both staff and students with his quiet involvement in every part of college life.

After two years of sometimes quite painful discussions, it was decided to merge GBC and Northumbria Bible College (formerly Lebanon Missionary Bible College), and, in recognition that this was a merger and not a take-over, it was decided to adopt the new name of International Christian College. ICC would continue with GBC's degree programme, with a few tweaks, to ensure continuity for the majority of students. That was not always easy for the NBC staff and Board to accept, but they recognised that to try to start over again with creating a new suite of courses would entail an enormous amount of work and would jeopardise the whole enterprise. The GBC degree was seen to be of a very high standard, and it would be hard to improve on it and get through all the complexities of accreditation in less than a couple more years. All staff from both institutions, however, were required to stand down, and to re-apply for each appointment, thus ensuring that whoever was best equipped for each post was the one to continue into the new body.

By now, GBC was already offering some postgraduate degrees, and with a higher proportion of staff with PhDs or other higher qualifications, plus a considerably larger team, it was inevitable that the majority of the new staff were from the GBC stream. They did not necessarily have more pastoral or ministry experience than the NBC staff, although all had some, including several with overseas experience. This situation was often hard for the NBC family to accept, however much they understood the rationale, and some had sore feelings for a long time. It helped that Peter Maiden, Chairman of the NBC Board, and international leader of Operation Mobilisation, became joint-chair of the new ICC Board with Colin Kirkwood representing GBC. Others from NBC did not wish to relocate from Berwick on Tweed, or were close to retirement and did not wish to start over again. David Smith, the principal of NBC, chose at that point to go to another ministry, in Oxford, but was later to join the ICC staff to lead a postgraduate course in urban mission. Among those who did transfer from NBC were Eryl Rowlands and Elizabeth Clark, who brought much valuable experience to the combined college. There were also new appointments of men and women who had been part of neither GBC nor NBC, and who came with fresh ideas. The joint Boards in 1998 invited Tony Sargent to become the next principal/first principal of ICC, leading through the first complex year of the actual merged body as it settled down, and then on till 2009. Tony was a graduate of London Bible College, who, for the previous 30 years before coming to Glasgow had been senior pastor of Worthing Tabernacle, a church which had grown considerably under his leadership. The Sussex coast in the very south of England is a far cry from urban Glasgow, but he soon settled in and adjusted to a very different ministry. He was also involved in relief and development projects in places as far-flung as India, Africa, and Eastern Europe, ensuring that along with his pastoral experience he also brought commitment to cross-cultural and missionary vocations. Sargent quickly became convinced that the Great Western Road former church building was constricting what the college could become. There had been many applications for some development of the building and of the site on which it stood: these had always been turned down by the City authorities, though 'miraculously' once ICC vacated the building a night club was able to acquire it and was immediately granted permission for considerable changes. It was an interesting reprise of the experience of leaving Bothwell Street a generation previously.

A search for an alternative home for ICC led to a building in St James Road, close to the northern boundary of Strathclyde University and also to the Royal Infirmary. It was also near the M8, and within easy walking distance from Queen Street Station and the nearby bus station. The building had been a nursing college and residence, linked to the hospital; but with the change to requiring nurses to have a university degree rather than simply on-the-job training, it was deemed to be no longer needed. Built over four stories it offered ample space for everything ICC wanted: several lecture halls, site for a spacious library, plenty of room for staff studies and for offices and meeting rooms, a big dining room (large enough for communal worship) and kitchen, some top-floor accommodation for residential students and for a warden, and room at the ground floor for several Christian ministries to rent space for their offices. It was a modern building, in good repair, unlikely to throw up expensive building repairs in the near future. It needed some adjustments to be made, but nothing major. It was light and attractive. It would be a good home, and it was sensed that this was where the Lord was leading.

It was an act of faith to trust God for the money needed to purchase it and fit it out, but miraculously it came. Some Trust Funds helped, being more willing to contribute to capital investment than to everyday running costs. A year after Sargent's arrival ICC moved in. In many ways it was a fresh start for everybody, and there was a sense of energy and expectation.

Tony Sargent encouraged and supported relief development and education ministries in India, Kenya, Uganda and Romania

37
The final lap

ONCE again, colleges numbers went up. There were many part-time students, and alongside the BA programmes, gradually a new suite of postgraduate options, such as Ministry in an Urban World, or Biblical Interpretation, or research degrees were all added. These were designed so that in most cases they could be combined with ongoing ministry or other occupations, while some courses were primarily full-time. Within a few years there were over 30 enrolled on the postgraduate courses. Previously validated by the Open University, by 2007 all undergraduate and postgraduate degrees were validated by the University of Aberdeen, demonstrating the confidence that institution had in the rigour and conduct of the academic programme. In due course, some students enrolled for PhD studies. David Smith, former principal at Northumbria Bible College, returned to ICC in 2002 to develop the courses, especially at postgraduate level, in Urban Ministry. David had pastored a church in Cambridge, and served some hugely formative years in Africa before landing at NBC as principal. He then spent four years in Oxford at what was then the Whitefield Institute, a research arm at that time of UCCF. Deeply concerned with the need to contextualise the gospel in a fast changing and swiftly urbanising world led him to ICC to design and lead a Masters that grappled with those issues. Placements took students – from several countries – to many countries, as far afield as Nairobi. In January 2008 David was joined by Wes White, who was to take over leadership of the course when David stepped down the following year.

The Youth Work course, had begun in 1998 at GBC under Neil Pratt, a former BTI/GBC student, who initially was seconded by the Oasis Trust. As ICC became established, this now developed markedly, evolving into a BA in Youth Work and Applied Theology. Students attended college a couple of days each week while embedded in an employing church or agency where they applied their training and practice. Quite a few churches were appointing youth workers as they saw the urgent need for concentrated work with children and young people, increasingly alienated from the churches. In 2004, the National Youth Agency recognised the course as qualification for youth and community work in the public sector, which brought openings way beyond the Christian sphere. The course was also validated by Aberdeen University. Pratt was later joined by Graeme McMeekin and by Julie Green.

Meanwhile, Vicki Shaver was focusing on ministry among children, and had led the design and practice of a BA in Theology with a strong thread of modules engaging specifically with the need to reach and disciple children. She had previously served for many years with Scripture Union, and during that time

had visited BTI/GBC for input about children's ministry. Her experience had taken her not only to situations across Scotland, but way beyond to contexts in several African countries. She brought wisdom and great gentle humour, with pastoral concern, to the staff team, including leading the BA Theology Programme overall for a couple of years. But it was the ministry to children that was most fully her heart passion, and it was infectious.

Richard Tiplady, ICC's last Principal 2010-14

There was also a succession of Americans who joined the staff team. Rick Hess had been an early arrival, in 1988, staying for six years during BTI/GBC years, before moving on first to London, then to Dallas, Texas, where he was appointed Professor in Old Testament. He married a Scottish GBC graduate, who had been one of his students, and drily remarked that he gained more than he gave while at the college! At ICC, in 1999 Darrell Cosden arrived to teach theology and Ethics. He had worked for some years in the former Soviet Union, and then completed a PhD in St Andrew's. He left after eight years to take up a Professorial post in Illinois, USA. In 2006, John Dennis came as lecturer in

New Testament. Wes White, mentioned above, had grown up in the Congo, the son of medical missionaries. After studies in the USA and 15 years as a church pastor, also in America, in 2001 he came to Glasgow and established a pioneer church plant, the Mosaic Community, seeking to reach those who did not feel at home in the established churches.

Not all the staff appointed were men! In addition to Vicki Shaver and Elizabeth Clark (who had come from NBC), Marion Carson strengthened the pastoral studies and counselling input, and shared her deep concern both for women in ministry and for the care of marginalised and abused women. Jane McArthur, another former BTI student who had gone on to further theological studies, became a much-appreciated lecturer in theology. Audrey Newton, whose husband Derek was leading the post-graduate course in Biblical Interpretation, taught some New Testament courses. These and other women associated with the college were vital role models of women in ministry. This was all the more important as some students came from churches where women were barred from any kind of leadership, at a time when some Scottish denominations were dividing acrimoniously over the issue.

In September 2008, Ted Herbert, who had been a much-loved lecturer at GBC and then continued as Vice-Principal of ICC from its beginning, died of cancer after a short illness. It was a blow to all the ICC community. Eryl Rowlands, who had served at NBC before the merger, and had been a steady hand in the new era, had actually retired, but came back to serve as an interim Vice-Principal. In due course, following Tony Sargent's retirement in 2009, the role was divided between two staff, David Miller and Graeme McMeekin. Miller had been a student at BTI, where he also met his wife, Jeannette, and then they had served for a long time in Japan. After post-graduate study in Edinburgh, Miller was appointed at GBC to lecture in Mission Studies, in succession to Rose Dowsett. McMeekin was by now leading the youth work team.

They led the college till the arrival soon after of Richard Tiplady, the new principal. Tiplady was yet another former BTI student, who had also met his wife, Irene, there. For some years, he had been serving with Global Connections, latterly leading it. Global Connections had its roots as the overseas missionary arm of the UK Evangelical Alliance, linking and resourcing a wide range of agencies, churches and individuals. Very conscious of the fast-changing British church scene, and of the changing role of western missionaries in the 21st century, Tiplady had helped many agencies in particular think about how to adjust to a new era, and to focus on new possibilities and responsibilities rather than retreating into irrelevance or unwillingness to change.

38
The last chapter

ICC also needed to face those challenges, and more besides.
There had been many students in the ICC years, who had fanned out into effective ministries in the UK and around the world. There was optimism and an ongoing commitment to the formation, under God, of men and women committed to the gospel, to the 'faith once delivered', and to faithful service. They were good years, despite the inevitable ups and downs. This generation of students are still in active ministry. It is perhaps not appropriate to name them, but suffice it to say that many Scottish churches, along with many others around the wider world, are currently benefiting greatly from these men and women.

While in the first years of ICC student numbers had been fairly high, before long falling numbers in the Scottish churches meant there were fewer domestic undergraduates applying to ICC, the UK-wide economic situation was suffering in the financial crash of 2008, and obtaining visas for non-EU would-be students became increasingly difficult and expensive and fewer were able to come. Even full sponsorship by someone in Scotland was sometimes deemed inadequate, and the applicant turned down by the visa authorities. Some churches were running their own small-scale apprenticeship programmes, with some supervised study included. Proclamation Trust started up in Glasgow. Shrinking congregations were appointing fewer staff, leaving fewer openings for employment for ICC graduates. Fewer people were willing to commit to service overseas except on a very short-term basis, for which training requirements were much reduced, and fewer churches were interested in supporting them.

In February 2008, the Scottish Government abolished university tuition fees for Scottish and EU students, while in England they were climbing steadily higher. While the support to Scottish universities to compensate for abolishing fees was supplied from central funds, no such help was available to independent colleges such as ICC, despite the fact that its degrees were validated by Aberdeen University. In England, Bible and Theological colleges could now keep their fees lower than university fees, or on a par with them; in Scotland it was cheaper to go to university for free than to pay ICC fees. Highland Theological College escaped this dilemma as it was part of the University of the Highlands and Islands. Over and above what ICC charged students, there was a shortfall of about £1,700 per (full-time) student per year, and already it caused considerable hardship for most students to raise their tuition costs plus living costs. Often family and churches would say it was now more 'moral' to go to a university theology/divinity department than to stack up large debts through paying ICC fees. Would-be students applied, were accepted, and then withdrew under pressure from family members, friends, or even pastors. Some 20% of needed income for the college came through gifts from friends of the college, but these never kept up with expenses. There were dwindling reserves, and without sharply increasing the number of students this could not be sustained. Many students had appreciated the range of course options available at both undergraduate and postgraduate levels, and the access to many staff pastorally; but the price had been the considerable expansion of the staff, both academic and administrative, to cover them all. The staff-student ratio could not be maintained.

The staff and Board worked very hard to find solutions. Would a different kind of course attract more students? Should some courses be wound up, as the experimental course GBC ran for a few years for Korean pastors keen to learn English and English theological language had to do? Valuable but not well enough attended. Were there too many postgraduate options? Again, with good rationale for each one, but most with small numbers on them. Should the college pull in its horns and move into much smaller premises and try to live even more frugally? What economies could be adopted without compromising academic standards? Some staff moved to part-time work, but it was not possible to carry the current workload this way indefinitely, and the pressure on all staff was huge. Student numbers continued to fall. Perhaps the jungle drums sent out the message that the college was in trouble, and nobody wanted to risk starting a course that might not be completed.

Finally, in 2014 it was announced that the college would close. Arrangements were made for existing students, part-way through their courses, to be able to transfer to another college or university to complete their programme. Some students were quite resentful of this turn of events, others were more philosophical or understanding. There was a very brief attempt at a new initiative in partnership with the Nazarene Theological College, based in Manchester, to set up a Scottish School of Christian Mission, focused entirely on equipping men and women for missional service within churches or through church plants or pioneering Christian communities in fresh forms. Sadly, it did not take off, and after a short while came to an end.

The BTI story had continued for more than 120 years. Now it was the end of an era.

39

A last word

WHEN I learned the college was closing, I wept.......and wept. It took me a very long time to come to terms with the closure. I had taught, first part-time and then full-time, in the 1980s and 90s, under Geoff Grogan and Peter White, both world church history and mission studies. So many students and staff became close friends, and it was always a great joy to follow them as they moved on into whatever ministry it was that the Lord had called them to, and shaped them for. Part of my heart was anchored in this community. Later I served for several years on the ICC Board. I rejoiced in all that God had done, both in the UK and around the world, through those who had been part of the story down through the many years since BTI's inception in 1892/3, and loved tracing the story of many an individual former student, from that long-ago beginning to the present.

Before he died in 2011, Geoff Grogan asked me to put some of those stories on paper. For various reasons, it has taken a decade to fulfil that request. I think he would have been deeply grieved at the college's closure, while perhaps understanding why that happened. It certainly made it harder to do as he asked, at least until some years had passed and given some measure of distance from the final painful chapter. Also, as archives were dispersed or even culled, and my own mobility decreased, it was difficult to trace some of the material I should like to have studied.

My own lifetime of involvement in world mission, and the encounter over and over again down through the years with former students scattered across the world, or with people on every continent who gave witness to the impact of BTI/GBC/ICC graduates on the church in their country, has meant that I have been especially interested in tracing some of that thread. In my own mission agency, OMF International, and its predecessor the China Inland Mission, hundreds of BTI and GBC graduates played a role in the growth of the church in Asia. I could have filled this volume with their stories alone, and in some ways it would have been easier as I have more access to that agency's archives. But I have tried to illustrate from the wider world, often dependent on personal letters. I have had to be selective about stories to tell; my apologies to anyone who feels hurt that their story did not appear.

In the goodness of the Lord, former students have played a considerable role in the birth and growth of the majority world churches, which now greatly outnumber northern Christians. Perhaps not many Scottish Christians today know about that great contribution, and I think it is important to put that on record. As for ministry within the UK, that has also been hugely significant, and all over the British Isles there are the footprints of men and women, trained through this college, who have helped shape many a congregation or agency, pastored and taught and reached out to those not yet believing, who have taught in schools and nursed in hospitals carrying the torch of the gospel, impacted communities or raised believing children, had hidden ministries or high-profile ones: only God himself knows the full story.

Sometimes the season for a particular ministry comes to an end. It does not invalidate what has been achieved through its lifetime. Perhaps a new generation of fresh ministries come into being in its place. Under God, the Bible College movement which emerged in many countries from the time Moody started his Institute in 1889 to the present has proved to be a movement blessed and used by God, for the extending of the Kingdom, and for its contribution to the establishing of today's' global Church.

As believing men and women would echo down through the years and around the world, 'To God be the Glory'.

Rose Dowsett
Milngavie, Glasgow, Scotland
2022